Pixelated Halloween Quilt

Toni Smith
Nicole Ellison

Quiltoni

Pixelated Halloween Quilt
Toni Smith & Nicole Ellison

Pixelated Halloween Quilt
Toni Smith & Nicole Ellison
OCTOBER 2022
Published by Quiltoni
PO Box 4763, Crofton, Md, 21114
©2022 by Quiltoni
ISBN 978-1-7322295-3-2
LCCN

Quiltoni

Table Of Contents
Pixelated Halloween Quilt

Welcome
to the
Pixelated Halloween Quilt

I had a quilty dream.

Could there be a quilt along that was entirely online, while partnering with quilt and sewing stores? Where each block released weekly for a small cost, but would be free if a participating store gave you the download code?

The answer to all of these questions turned out to be yes! The quilt along was a resounding success, so we decided to do it again! This time we created a Halloween themed quilt along and this book is the result. Each block includes instructions for creating it as part of the quilt, or as a stand alone piece.

If you need help along the way, I have tutorials for all of the techniques at youtube.com/quiltoni.

Pixelated Halloween - A Spoopy Quilt-a-long

Suggested Fabrics for this project are from the Toscana line by Northcott Fabrics

Color Name	Fabric Swatch	Color Name	Fabric Swatch
Black	Ebony 9020-99	Orange	Monarch 9020-571
White	Pickett Fence 9020-10	Light Yellow	Custard 9020-530
Light Blue	Blue Moon 9020-43	Dark Blue	Lapis 9020-472
Brown	Sponge Toffee 9020-350	Apple Green	Par 4 9020-733
Purple	Iris 9020-835	Light Gray	Going Gray 9020-93
Dark Gray	Evening Shadow 9020-95	Sashing Fabric	Ebony 9020-99 (Used in Sample)

PIXELATED HALLOWEEN

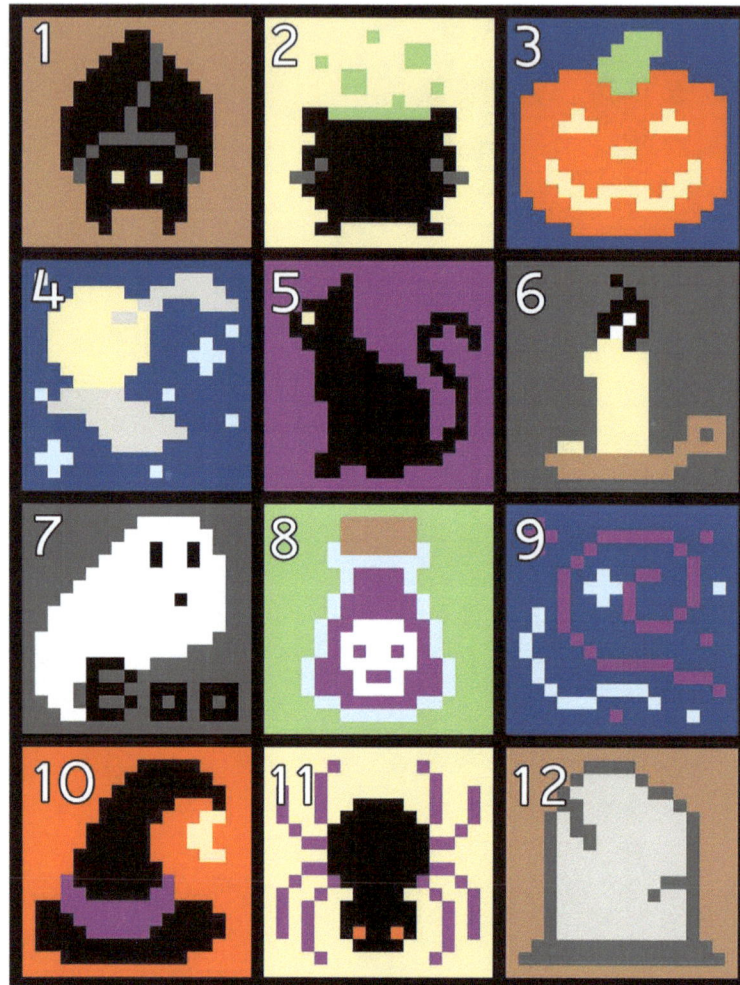

Block Description	Block Number	Fabric Colors Required
Bat	1	Black, Dark Gray, Light Yellow, Brown
Cauldron	2	Black, Dark Gray, Light Yellow, Apple Green
Jack-o-Lantern	3	Dark Blue, Orange, Light Yellow, Apple Green
Full Moon	4	Dark Blue, Light Yellow, Light Gray, Light Blue
Black Cat	5	Black, Purple, Light Yellow
Black Flame Candle	6	Black, White, Light Yellow, Brown, Dark Gray
Ghost	7	White, Black, Dark Gray
Poison Bottle	8	White, Apple Green, Light Blue, Brown, Purple
Magic	9	Dark Blue, Light Blue, Purple
Magic Hat	10	Black, Orange, Purple, Light Yellow
Spider	11	Black, Purple, Light Yellow, Orange
Tombstone	12	Brown, Dark Gray, Light Gray

(2)

FABRIC COLOR & NAME	TOTAL YARDAGE	USED IN THESE BLOCKS
WHITE	¾ YARD	6, 7, 8
BLACK	1 ½ YARDS	1, 2, 5, 6, 7, 10, 11
ORANGE	¾ YARD	3, 10, 11
LIGHT YELLOW	1 ¼ YARDS	1, 2, 3, 4, 5, 6, 10, 11
APPLE GREEN	¾ YARD	2, 3, 8
LIGHT BLUE	¼ YARD	4, 8, 9
DARK BLUE	1 ½ YARDS	3, 4, 9
PURPLE	¾ YARD	5, 8, 9, 10, 11
BROWN	1 YARD	1, 6, 8, 12
LIGHT GRAY	½ YARD	4, 12
DARK GRAY	1 YARD	1, 2, 6, 7, 12
SASHING FABRIC	1 ½ YARDS	SASHING

YARDAGE QUOTED HERE IS INTENDED FOR THE ENTIRE QUILT.

WHEN SHOPPING FOR YOUR FABRIC, PLEASE KEEP THE BLOCKS IN MIND THAT THE FABRIC WILL BE USED FOR.

IF YOU ARE ONLY MAKING A FEW OF THE BLOCKS, PLEASE REFER TO THE INDIVIDUAL BLOCK INSTRUCTIONS FOR THE SPECIFIC YARDAGE.

FINAL MEASUREMENTS FOR THE FINISHED 12 BLOCK QUILT IS 70.5" BY 92.5"

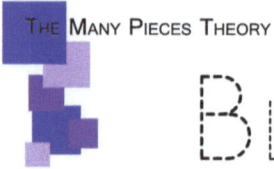

BLOCK 1
- BAT

FINISHED BLOCK MEASURES 18" BY 18".

TEXT IN A HIGHLIGHTED BLOCK INDICATES A QUILTING TIP AND CAN BE SKIPPED BY EXPERIENCED QUILTERS.

BEFORE CUTTING STRIPS OF FABRIC, MAKE SURE YOUR FABRIC IS WASHED AND IRONED. CUT STRIPS FROM SELVAGE TO SELVAGE (ALONG THE LENGTH SO STRIPS ARE ALWAYS A MINIMUM OF 40 INCHES) USING A ROTARY CUTTER AND A STRAIGHT EDGE. ALWAYS TRIM THE SELVAGE BEFORE YOU BEGIN CUTTING A NEW FABRIC AND USE A ¼ INCH SEAM WHEN SEWING TOGETHER FABRICS. THE "RIGHT" SIDE OF THE FABRIC IS THE ONE WITH THE DESIGN OR MOST COLOR. THE "WRONG" SIDE IS THE BACK OF THE FABRIC.

IF YOU ARE MAKING THIS BLOCK AS A STANDALONE AND NOT PART OF THE PIXELATED HALLOWEEN QUILT A LONG, ½ YARD OF BLACK AND BROWN FABRIC AND ¼ YARD OF DARK GRAY AND LIGHT YELLOW FABRIC ARE NEEDED.

1) CUT THE FOLLOWING FABRICS:

	COLOR	2½" STRIP	1½" STRIP
	BLACK	2	3
	BROWN	3	2
	DARK GRAY	1	2
	LIGHT YELLOW	0	1

SET ASIDE ALL OF THE 1½" STRIPS.

WITH THE 2½" STRIPS:
FROM THE BLACK FABRIC CUT (4) 2½" X 4½" RECTANGLES AND (10) 2½" X 2½" SQUARES

FROM THE BROWN FABRIC CUT (15) 2½" X 4½" RECTANGLES, (10) 2½" X 2½" SQUARES,

AND (3) 2½" X 1½" RECTANGLES

FROM THE DARK GRAY FABRIC CUT (1) 2½" X 1½" RECTANGLE

SET THESE PIECES ASIDE.

(4)

2) Using the 1½" strips, sew the right sides together for each of the following combinations:

1 Black Strip to 1 Brown Strip
1 Black Strip to 1 Dark Gray Strip
1 Black Strip to 1 Light Yellow Strip
1 Brown Strip to 1 Dark Gray Strip

Cut each of these newly combined strips in half.

Iron each half of the strips open in opposite directions. For example, iron half of the Brown/Dark Gray strip towards the Brown and the other half towards the Dark Gray. These new strips should now measure 2½" in width.

3) Take the Brown/Dark Gray strips and nest the seams (lining the seams up in opposite directions to allow the fabric to line up perfectly) by laying one right side up and the other wrong side up on top of it. Line your strips up evenly and trim the edge.

Top View: Side View:

Then cut (1) set of 2 ½" x 1 ½" rectangles (2 total)

Repeat this process for each set of strips cutting:

Black/Brown - (4) sets of 2½" x 2½" squares (8 total),   (4) sets of 2½" x 1½" rectangles (8 total)

Black/Dark Gray - (2) sets of 2½" x 2½" squares (4 total),   (5) sets of 2½" x 1½" rectangles (10 total)

Black/Light Yellow - (1) set of 2½" x 1½" rectangles (2 total)

4) Now it is time to lay out all of the pieces. Start with the first row and lay each piece right side up, making sure you pay attention to the direction the seam is facing. Always make sure the seam is facing the direction of the arrow. If the seam is facing up or down, make sure that the piece next to it is nested (has the seam in the opposite direction). Re-iron any seams that need to be changed to a different direction.

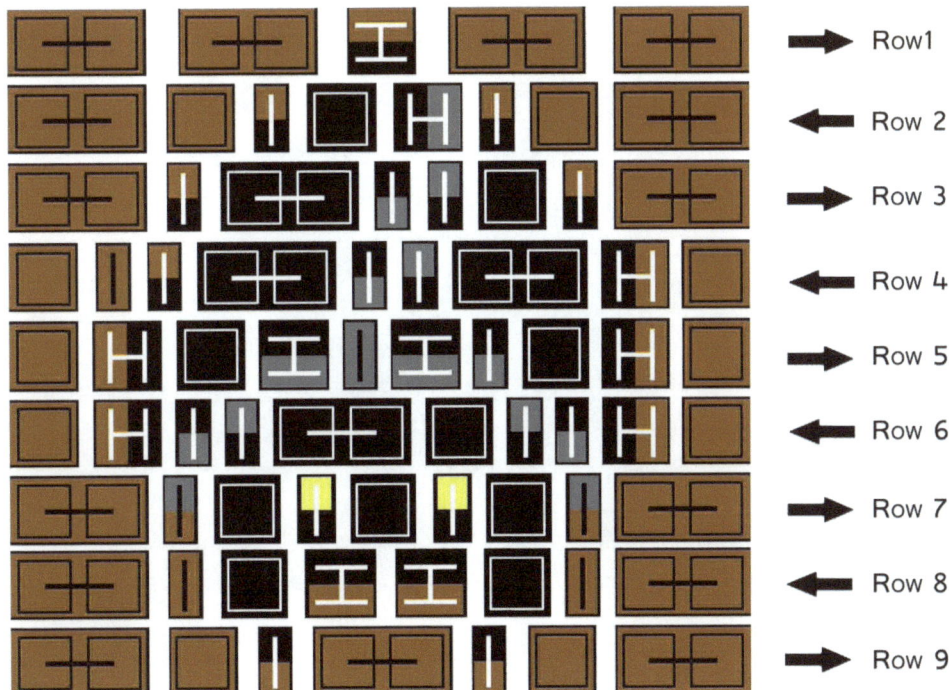

Row 1 →
Row 2 ←
Row 3 →
Row 4 ←
Row 5 →
Row 6 ←
Row 7 →
Row 8 ←
Row 9 →

(5)

5) Assemble each row, sewing right sides together and seams facing the direction of the arrow.

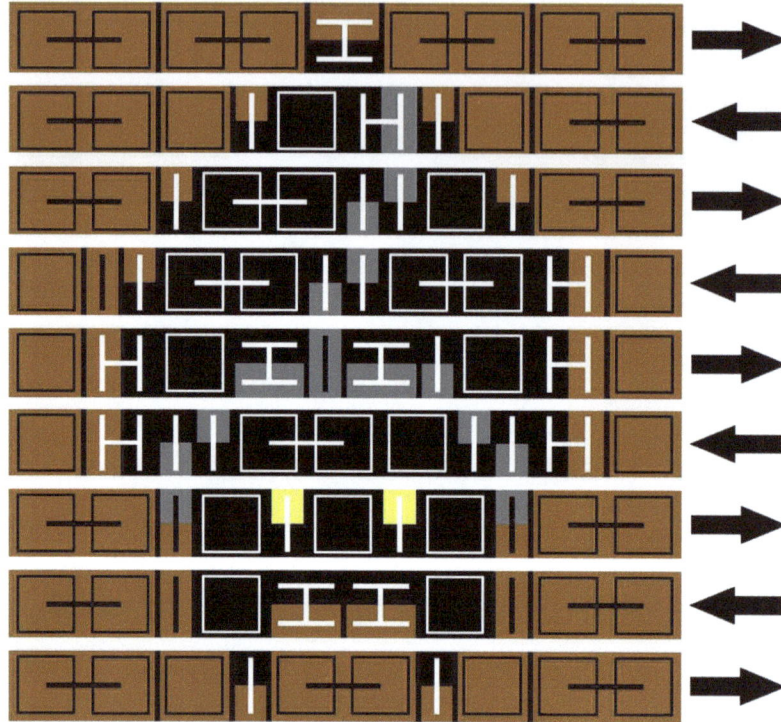

6) Sew the rows together, it does not matter which direction your seams point.

7) "Square" your block. Trim the edges of your block so they are even and your block is 18" by 18".

8) If this block is being made as part of the Pixelated Halloween Quilt a Long, set aside any fabric and combined strips you didn't use for future blocks.

(6)

BLOCK 2 -- CAULDRON

FINISHED BLOCK MEASURES 18" BY 18".

TEXT IN A HIGHLIGHTED BLOCK INDICATES A QUILTING TIP AND CAN BE SKIPPED BY EXPERIENCED QUILTERS.

BEFORE CUTTING STRIPS OF FABRIC, MAKE SURE YOUR FABRIC IS WASHED AND IRONED. CUT STRIPS FROM SELVAGE TO SELVAGE (ALONG THE LENGTH SO STRIPS ARE ALWAYS A MINIMUM OF 40 INCHES) USING A ROTARY CUTTER AND A STRAIGHT EDGE. ALWAYS TRIM THE SELVAGE BEFORE YOU BEGIN CUTTING A NEW FABRIC AND USE A ¼ INCH SEAM WHEN SEWING TOGETHER FABRICS. THE "RIGHT" SIDE OF THE FABRIC IS THE ONE WITH THE DESIGN OR MOST COLOR. THE "WRONG" SIDE IS THE BACK OF THE FABRIC.

IF YOU ARE MAKING THIS BLOCK AS A STANDALONE AND NOT PART OF THE PIXELATED HALLOWEEN QUILT A LONG, ½ YARD OF LIGHT YELLOW FABRIC AND ¼ YARD OF BLACK, DARK GRAY AND APPLE GREEN FABRIC ARE NEEDED.

IF THIS BLOCK IS BEING MADE AS PART OF THE PIXELATED HALLOWEEN QUILT A LONG, USE THE FOLLOWING STRIPS FROM PREVIOUS BLOCKS (AND DO NOT CUT ADDITIONAL STRIPS OF THEM, DEDUCT THIS NUMBER OF STRIPS FROM THE CHART BELOW):
(1) BLACK 2 ½" STRIP
(1) DARK GRAY 2½" STRIP
BLACK/DARK GRAY COMBINED STRIP (DO NOT CUT 1 OF THE 1½" STRIPS OF EACH COLOR)
BLACK/LIGHT YELLOW COMBINED STRIP (DO NOT CUT 1 OF THE 1½" STRIPS OF EACH COLOR)

1) CUT THE FOLLOWING FABRICS:

COLOR		2½" STRIP	1½" STRIP
■	BLACK	2	2
■	DARK GRAY	1	1
■	LIGHT YELLOW	3	2
■	APPLE GREEN	1	1

SET ASIDE ALL OF THE 1½" STRIPS.
WITH THE 2½" STRIPS:
FROM THE BLACK FABRIC CUT (8) 2½" x 4½" RECTANGLES AND (2) 2½" x 2½" SQUARES

FROM THE DARK GRAY FABRIC CUT (2) 2 ½ " x 1 ½" RECTANGLES

FROM THE LIGHT YELLOW FABRIC CUT (15) 2 ½ " x 4 ½" RECTANGLES, (11) 2 ½" x 2 ½" SQUARES,

AND (7) 2 ½ " x 1 ½" RECTANGLES

FROM THE APPLE GREEN FABRIC CUT (2) 2 ½" x 2 ½" SQUARES, AND (1) 2 ½ " x 1 ½" RECTANGLE

SET THESE PIECES ASIDE.

(7)

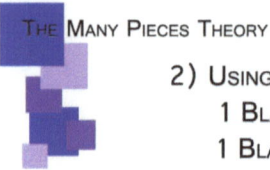

2) USING THE 1½" STRIPS, SEW THE RIGHT SIDES TOGETHER FOR EACH OF THE FOLLOWING COMBINATIONS:

1 BLACK STRIP TO 1 DARK GRAY STRIP
1 BLACK STRIP TO 1 LIGHT YELLOW STRIP
1 LIGHT YELLOW STRIP TO 1 APPLE GREEN STRIP

CUT EACH OF THESE NEWLY COMBINED STRIPS IN HALF.

IRON EACH HALF OF THE STRIPS OPEN IN OPPOSITE DIRECTIONS. FOR EXAMPLE, IRON HALF OF THE LIGHTT YELLOW/APPLE GREEN STRIP TOWARDS THE LIGHT YELLOW AND THE OTHER HALF TOWARDS THE APPLE GREEN. THESE NEW STRIPS SHOULD NOW MEASURE 2½" IN WIDTH.

3) TAKE THE LIGHT YELLOW/APPLE GREEN STRIPS AND NEST THE SEAMS (LINING THE SEAMS UP IN OPPOSITE DIRECTIONS TO ALLOW THE FABRIC TO LINE UP PERFECTLY) BY LAYING ONE RIGHT SIDE UP AND THE OTHER WRONG SIDE UP ON TOP OF IT. LINE YOUR STRIPS UP EVENLY AND TRIM THE EDGE.

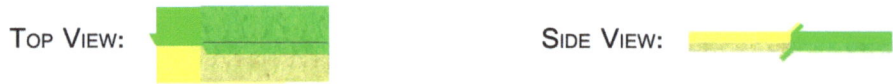

TOP VIEW: SIDE VIEW:

THEN CUT (2) SETS OF 2 ½" x 2 ½" SQUARES (4 TOTAL),   (2) SETS OF 2 ½" x 1 ½" RECTANGLES (4 TOTAL)

REPEAT THIS PROCESS FOR EACH SET OF STRIPS CUTTING:

BLACK/DARK GRAY - (1) SET OF 2 ½" x 1 ½" RECTANGLES (2 TOTAL)

BLACK/LIGHT YELLOW - (3) SETS OF 2 ½" x 2 ½" SQUARES (6 TOTAL),

(3) SETS OF 2 ½" x 1 ½" RECTANGLES (6 TOTAL)

4) NOW IT IS TIME TO LAY OUT ALL OF THE PIECES. START WITH THE FIRST ROW AND LAY EACH PIECE RIGHT SIDE UP, MAKING SURE YOU PAY ATTENTION TO THE DIRECTION THE SEAM IS FACING. ALWAYS MAKE SURE THE SEAM IS FACING THE DIRECTION OF THE ARROW. IF THE SEAM IS FACING UP OR DOWN, MAKE SURE THAT THE PIECE NEXT TO IT IS NESTED (HAS THE SEAM IN THE OPPOSITE DIRECTION). RE-IRON ANY SEAMS THAT NEED TO BE CHANGED TO A DIFFERENT DIRECTION.

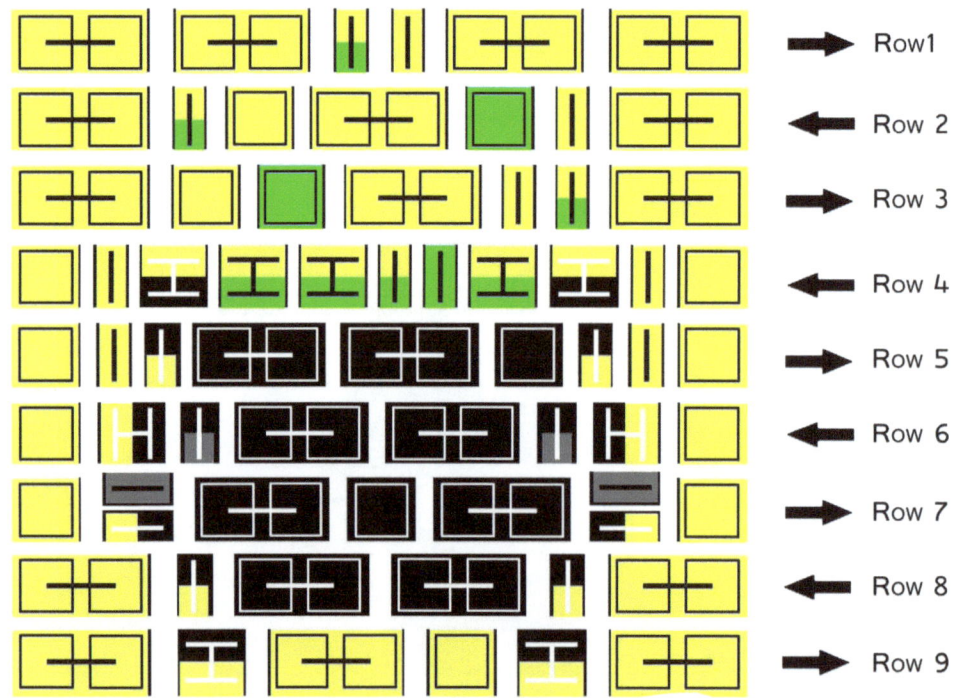

→ Row1

← Row 2

→ Row 3

← Row 4

→ Row 5

← Row 6

→ Row 7

← Row 8

→ Row 9

5) SEW TOGETHER THE TWO PIECES THAT NEED TO BE ASSEMBLED HORIZONTALLY.

Row 7

6) ASSEMBLE EACH ROW, SEWING RIGHT SIDES TOGETHER AND SEAMS FACING THE DIRECTION OF THE ARROW.

7) SEW THE ROWS TOGETHER, IT DOES NOT MATTER WHICH DIRECTION YOUR SEAMS POINT.

8) "SQUARE" YOUR BLOCK. TRIM THE EDGES OF YOUR BLOCK SO THEY ARE EVEN AND YOUR BLOCK IS 18" BY 18".

9) IF THIS BLOCK IS BEING MADE AS PART OF THE PIXELATED HALLOWEEN QUILT A LONG, SET ASIDE ANY FABRIC AND COMBINED STRIPS YOU DIDN'T USE FOR FUTURE BLOCKS.

BLOCK 3 - PUMPKIN

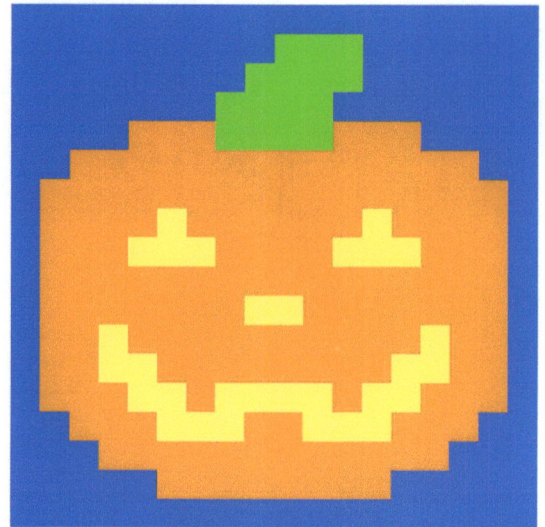

FINISHED BLOCK MEASURES 18" BY 18".

TEXT IN A HIGHLIGHTED BLOCK INDICATES A QUILTING TIP AND CAN BE SKIPPED BY EXPERIENCED QUILTERS.

BEFORE CUTTING STRIPS OF FABRIC, MAKE SURE YOUR FABRIC IS WASHED AND IRONED. CUT STRIPS FROM SELVAGE TO SELVAGE (ALONG THE LENGTH SO STRIPS ARE ALWAYS A MINIMUM OF 40 INCHES) USING A ROTARY CUTTER AND A STRAIGHT EDGE. ALWAYS TRIM THE SELVAGE BEFORE YOU BEGIN CUTTING A NEW FABRIC AND USE A ¼ INCH SEAM WHEN SEWING TOGETHER FABRICS. THE "RIGHT" SIDE OF THE FABRIC IS THE ONE WITH THE DESIGN OR MOST COLOR. THE "WRONG" SIDE IS THE BACK OF THE FABRIC.

IF YOU ARE MAKING THIS BLOCK AS A STANDALONE AND NOT PART OF THE PIXELATED HALLOWEEN QUILT A LONG, ¼ YARD OF ORANGE, LIGHT YELLOW, DARK BLUE AND APPLE GREEN FABRIC ARE NEEDED.

IF THIS BLOCK IS BEING MADE AS PART OF THE PIXELATED HALLOWEEN QUILT A LONG, USE THE FOLLOWING STRIPS FROM PREVIOUS BLOCKS (AND DO NOT CUT ADDITIONAL STRIPS OF THEM, DEDUCT THIS NUMBER OF STRIPS FROM THE CHART BELOW):
1 APPLE GREEN 2 ½" STRIP
1 LIGHT YELLOW 2 ½" STRIP

1) CUT THE FOLLOWING FABRICS:

	COLOR	2½" STRIP	1½" STRIP
	ORANGE	2	2
	LIGHT YELLOW	1	1
	DARK BLUE	3	2
	APPLE GREEN	1	1

SET ASIDE ALL OF THE 1½" STRIPS.

WITH THE 2½" STRIPS:

FROM THE ORANGE FABRIC CUT (6) 2½ " X 4½" RECTANGLES, (12) 2½" X 2½" SQUARES AND (6) 2½ " X 1½" RECTANGLES

FROM THE LIGHT YELLOW FABRIC CUT (2) 2½ " X 1½" RECTANGLES

FROM THE DARK BLUE FABRIC CUT (7) 2 ½ " X 4 ½" RECTANGLES, (7) 2 ½ " X 2 ½" SQUARES, AND (10) 2 ½ " X 1 ½" RECTANGLES

FROM THE APPLE GREEN FABRIC CUT (1) 2 ½" X 2 ½" SQUARE, AND (3) 2 ½ " X 1 ½" RECTANGLES

SET THESE PIECES ASIDE.

(10)

2) USING THE 1½" STRIPS, SEW THE RIGHT SIDES TOGETHER FOR EACH OF THE FOLLOWING COMBINATIONS:

1 ORANGE STRIP TO 1 DARK BLUE STRIP
1 ORANGE STRIP TO 1 LIGHT YELLOW STRIP
1 DARK BLUE STRIP TO 1 APPLE GREEN STRIP
CUT EACH OF THESE NEWLY COMBINED STRIPS IN HALF.

IRON EACH HALF OF THE STRIPS OPEN IN OPPOSITE DIRECTIONS. FOR EXAMPLE, IRON HALF OF THE ORANGE/DARK BLUE STRIP TOWARDS THE ORANGE AND THE OTHER HALF TOWARDS THE DARK BLUE. THESE NEW STRIPS SHOULD NOW MEASURE 2½" IN WIDTH.

3) TAKE THE ORANGE/DARK BLUE STRIPS AND NEST THE SEAMS (LINING THE SEAMS UP IN OPPOSITE DIRECTIONS TO ALLOW THE FABRIC TO LINE UP PERFECTLY) BY LAYING ONE RIGHT SIDE UP AND THE OTHER WRONG SIDE UP ON TOP OF IT. LINE YOUR STRIPS UP EVENLY AND TRIM THE EDGE.

TOP VIEW: SIDE VIEW:

THEN CUT (4) SETS OF 2½" x 2½" SQUARES (8 TOTAL),   (6) SETS OF 2½" x 1½" RECTANGLES (12 TOTAL)

REPEAT THIS PROCESS FOR EACH SET OF STRIPS CUTTING:

ORANGE/LIGHT YELLOW - (4) SETS OF 2½" x 2½" SQUARES (8 TOTAL),

(6) SETS OF 2½" x 1½" RECTANGLES (12 TOTAL)

DARK BLUE/APPLE GREEN - (1) SET OF 2½" x 2½" SQUARES (2 TOTAL),

(2) SETS OF 2½" x 1½" RECTANGLES (4 TOTAL)
SET ANY EXTRA PIECES ASIDE FOR FUTURE BLOCKS.

4) NOW IT IS TIME TO LAY OUT ALL OF THE PIECES. START WITH THE FIRST ROW AND LAY EACH PIECE RIGHT SIDE UP, MAKING SURE YOU PAY ATTENTION TO THE DIRECTION THE SEAM IS FACING. ALWAYS MAKE SURE THE SEAM IS FACING THE DIRECTION OF THE ARROW. IF THE SEAM IS FACING UP OR DOWN, MAKE SURE THAT THE PIECE NEXT TO IT IS NESTED (HAS THE SEAM IN THE OPPOSITE DIRECTION). RE-IRON ANY SEAMS THAT NEED TO BE CHANGED TO A DIFFERENT DIRECTION.

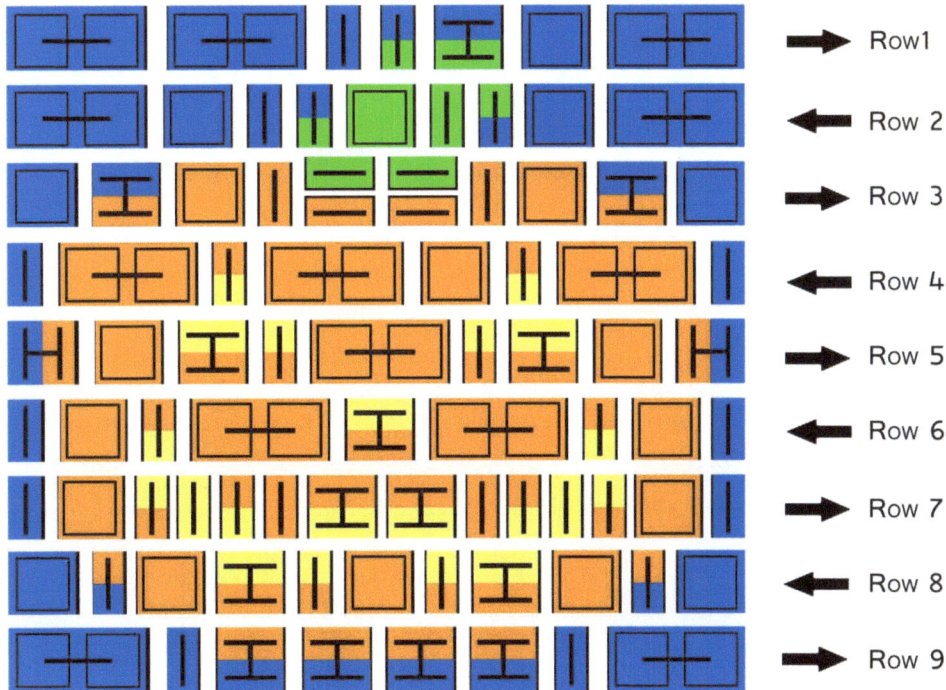

Row1

Row 2

Row 3

Row 4

Row 5

Row 6

Row 7

Row 8

Row 9

(11)

5) SEW TOGETHER THE TWO PIECES THAT NEED TO BE ASSEMBLED HORIZONTALLY.

Row 3

6) ASSEMBLE EACH ROW, SEWING RIGHT SIDES TOGETHER AND SEAMS FACING THE DIRECTION OF THE ARROW.

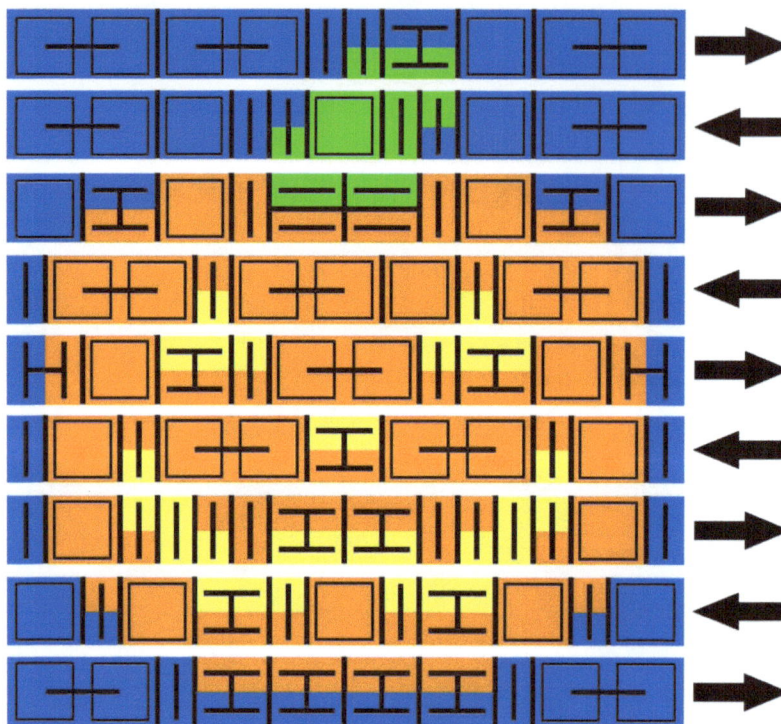

7) SEW THE ROWS TOGETHER, IT DOES NOT MATTER WHICH DIRECTION YOUR SEAMS POINT.

8) "SQUARE" YOUR BLOCK. TRIM THE EDGES OF YOUR BLOCK SO THEY ARE EVEN AND YOUR BLOCK IS 18" BY 18".

9) IF THIS BLOCK IS BEING MADE AS PART OF THE PIXELATED HALLOWEEN QUILT A LONG, SET ASIDE ANY FABRIC AND COMBINED STRIPS YOU DIDN'T USE FOR FUTURE BLOCKS.

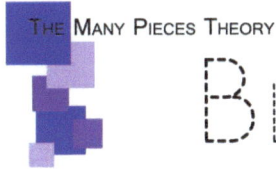

BLOCK 4 -- FULL MOON

FINISHED BLOCK MEASURES 18" BY 18".

TEXT IN A HIGHLIGHTED BLOCK INDICATES A QUILTING TIP AND CAN BE SKIPPED BY EXPERIENCED QUILTERS.

BEFORE CUTTING STRIPS OF FABRIC, MAKE SURE YOUR FABRIC IS WASHED AND IRONED. CUT STRIPS FROM SELVAGE TO SELVAGE (ALONG THE LENGTH SO STRIPS ARE ALWAYS A MINIMUM OF 40 INCHES) USING A ROTARY CUTTER AND A STRAIGHT EDGE. ALWAYS TRIM THE SELVAGE BEFORE YOU BEGIN CUTTING A NEW FABRIC AND USE A ¼ INCH SEAM WHEN SEWING TOGETHER FABRICS. THE "RIGHT" SIDE OF THE FABRIC IS THE ONE WITH THE DESIGN OR MOST COLOR. THE "WRONG" SIDE IS THE BACK OF THE FABRIC.

IF YOU ARE MAKING THIS BLOCK AS A STANDALONE AND NOT PART OF THE PIXELATED HALLOWEEN QUILT A LONG, ½ YARD OF DARK BLUE FABRIC AND ¼ YARD OF LIGHT BLUE, LIGHT YELLOW AND LIGHT GRAY FABRIC ARE NEEDED.

1) CUT THE FOLLOWING FABRICS:

	COLOR	2½" STRIP	1½" STRIP
	LIGHT BLUE	1	1
	LIGHT YELLOW	1	1
	DARK BLUE	3	2
	DARK GRAY	1	1

FROM THE 1½" STRIPS:
CUT 1 LIGHT BLUE STRIP, 1 LIGHT YELLOW STRIP AND 1 DARK BLUE STRIP IN HALF. SET THESE PIECES ASIDE.

WITH THE 2½" STRIPS:
FROM THE LIGHT BLUE FABRIC CUT (2) 2½" x 1½" RECTANGLES

FROM THE LIGHT YELLOW FABRIC CUT (5) 2½" x 4½" RECTANGLES AND (3) 2½" x 1½" RECTANGLES

FROM THE DARK BLUE FABRIC CUT (9) 2½" x 4½" RECTANGLES, (17) 2½" x 2½" SQUARES,

AND (19) 2½" x 1½" RECTANGLES

FROM THE LIGHT GRAY FABRIC CUT (2) 2½" x 4½" RECTANGLES, (2) 2½" x 2½" SQUARES,

AND (3) 2½" x 1½" RECTANGLES

SET THESE PIECES ASIDE.

(13)

2) USING THE 1½" STRIPS, SEW THE RIGHT SIDES TOGETHER FOR EACH OF THE FOLLOWING COMBINATIONS:
   ½ LIGHT BLUE STRIP TO ½ DARK BLUE STRIP
   ½ LIGHT YELLOW STRIP TO ½ DARK BLUE STRIP
   1 DARK BLUE STRIP TO 1 LIGHT GRAY STRIP
   CUT EACH OF THESE NEWLY COMBINED STRIPS IN HALF.

IRON EACH HALF OF THE STRIPS OPEN IN OPPOSITE DIRECTIONS. FOR EXAMPLE, IRON HALF OF THE LIGHT BLUE/DARK BLUE STRIP TOWARDS THE LIGHT BLUE AND THE OTHER HALF TOWARDS THE DARK BLUE. THESE NEW STRIPS SHOULD NOW MEASURE 2½" IN WIDTH.

3) TAKE THE LIGHT BLUE/DARK BLUE STRIPS AND NEST THE SEAMS (LINING THE SEAMS UP IN OPPOSITE DIRECTIONS TO ALLOW THE FABRIC TO LINE UP PERFECTLY) BY LAYING ONE RIGHT SIDE UP AND THE OTHER WRONG SIDE UP ON TOP OF IT. LINE YOUR STRIPS UP EVENLY AND TRIM THE EDGE.

TOP VIEW: SIDE VIEW:

THEN CUT (6) SETS OF 2½" X 1½" RECTANGLES (12 TOTAL)

REPEAT THIS PROCESS FOR EACH SET OF STRIPS CUTTING:
LIGHT YELLOW/DARK BLUE - (2) SETS OF 2½" X 1½" RECTANGLES (4 TOTAL)

DARK BLUE/LIGHT GRAY - (3) SETS OF 2½" X 2½" SQUARES (6 TOTAL)

(4) SETS OF 2½" X 1½" RECTANGLES (8 TOTAL)

SET ANY EXTRA PIECES ASIDE FOR FUTURE BLOCKS.

4) NOW IT IS TIME TO LAY OUT ALL OF THE PIECES. START WITH THE FIRST ROW AND LAY EACH PIECE RIGHT SIDE UP, MAKING SURE YOU PAY ATTENTION TO THE DIRECTION THE SEAM IS FACING. ALWAYS MAKE SURE THE SEAM IS FACING THE DIRECTION OF THE ARROW. IF THE SEAM IS FACING UP OR DOWN, MAKE SURE THAT THE PIECE NEXT TO IT IS NESTED (HAS THE SEAM IN THE OPPOSITE DIRECTION). RE-IRON ANY SEAMS THAT NEED TO BE CHANGED TO A DIFFERENT DIRECTION.

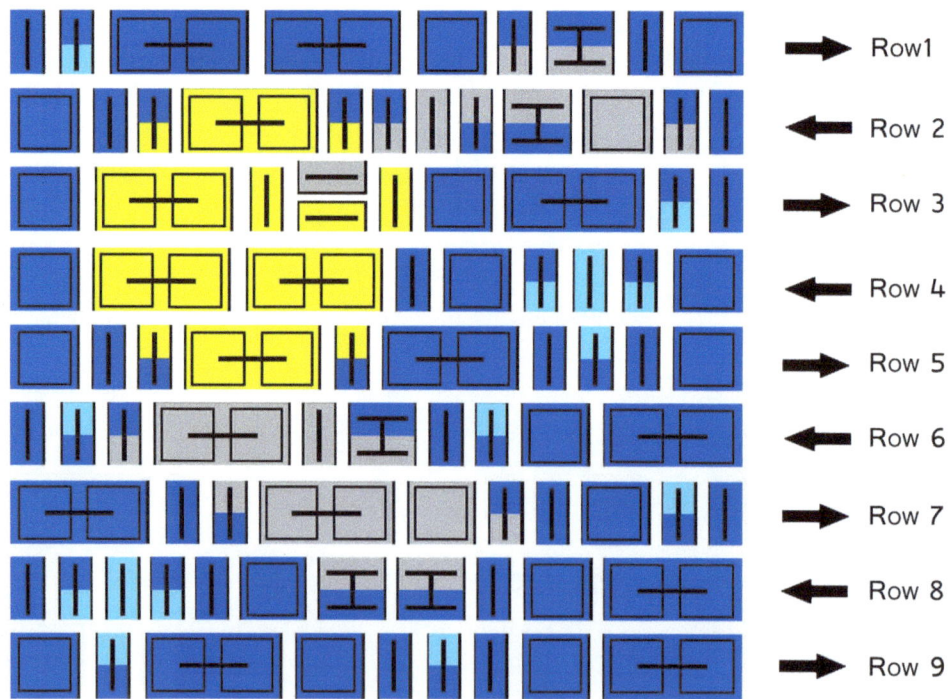

Row1 →
← Row 2
Row 3 →
← Row 4
Row 5 →
← Row 6
Row 7 →
← Row 8
Row 9 →

(14)

5) SEW TOGETHER THE ONE PIECE THAT NEED TO BE ASSEMBLED HORIZONTALLY.

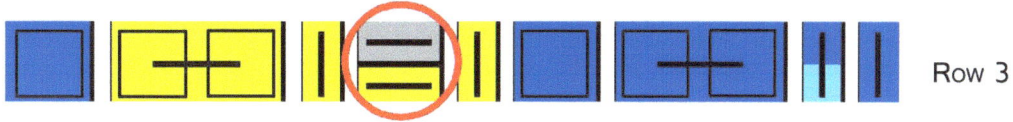

Row 3

6) ASSEMBLE EACH ROW, SEWING RIGHT SIDES TOGETHER AND SEAMS FACING THE DIRECTION OF THE ARROW.

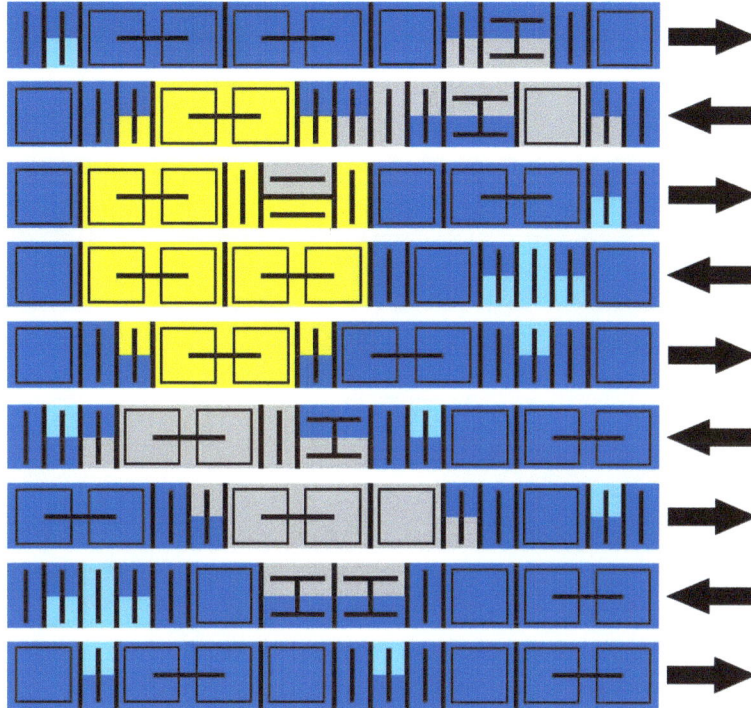

7) SEW THE ROWS TOGETHER, IT DOES NOT MATTER WHICH DIRECTION YOUR SEAMS POINT.

8) "SQUARE" YOUR BLOCK. TRIM THE EDGES OF YOUR BLOCK SO THEY ARE EVEN AND YOUR BLOCK IS 18" BY 18".

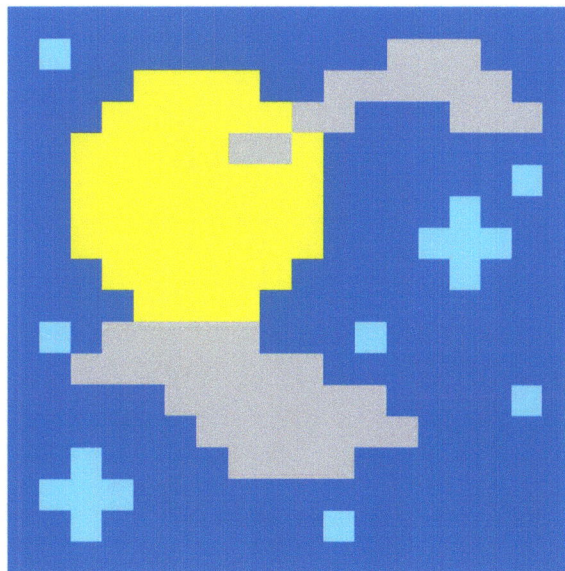

9) IF THIS BLOCK IS BEING MADE AS PART OF THE PIXELATED HALLOWEEN QUILT A LONG, SET ASIDE ANY FABRIC AND COMBINED STRIPS YOU DIDN'T USE FOR FUTURE BLOCKS.

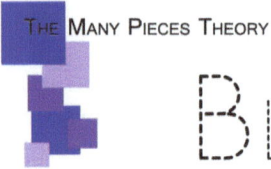

Block 5 -- Cat

Finished block measures 18" by 18".

TEXT IN A HIGHLIGHTED BLOCK INDICATES A QUILTING TIP AND CAN BE SKIPPED BY EXPERIENCED QUILTERS.

BEFORE CUTTING STRIPS OF FABRIC, MAKE SURE YOUR FABRIC IS WASHED AND IRONED. CUT STRIPS FROM SELVAGE TO SELVAGE (ALONG THE LENGTH SO STRIPS ARE ALWAYS A MINIMUM OF 40 INCHES) USING A ROTARY CUTTER AND A STRAIGHT EDGE. ALWAYS TRIM THE SELVAGE BEFORE YOU BEGIN CUTTING A NEW FABRIC AND USE A ¼ INCH SEAM WHEN SEWING TOGETHER FABRICS. THE "RIGHT" SIDE OF THE FABRIC IS THE ONE WITH THE DESIGN OR MOST COLOR. THE "WRONG" SIDE IS THE BACK OF THE FABRIC.

IF YOU ARE MAKING THIS BLOCK AS A STANDALONE AND NOT PART OF THE PIXELATED HALLOWEEN QUILT A LONG, ¼ YARD OF BLACK, PURPLE AND LIGHT YELLOW FABRIC ARE NEEDED.

IF THIS BLOCK IS BEING MADE AS PART OF THE PIXELATED HALLOWEEN QUILT A LONG, USE THE FOLLOWING STRIPS FROM PREVIOUS BLOCKS (AND DO NOT CUT ADDITIONAL STRIPS OF THEM, DEDUCT THIS NUMBER OF STRIPS FROM THE CHART BELOW):

(1) BLACK 2 ½" STRIP

BLACK/LIGHT YELLOW COMBINED STRIP (DO NOT CUT 1 OF THE 1 ½" STRIPS OF EACH COLOR)

1) CUT THE FOLLOWING FABRICS:

COLOR		2½" STRIP	1½" STRIP
■	BLACK	2	2
■	PURPLE	3	1
■	LIGHT YELLOW	0	1

SET ASIDE ALL OF THE 1½" STRIPS.

WITH THE 2½" STRIPS:

FROM THE BLACK FABRIC CUT (8) 2½" x 4½" RECTANGLE,   (3) 2½" x 2½" SQUARES,

AND (8) 2 ½" x 1 ½" RECTANGLES

FROM THE PURPLE FABRIC CUT (12) 2½" x 4½" RECTANGLE,   (15) 2 ½" x 2 ½" SQUARES,

AND (11) 2½" x 1½" RECTANGLES

SET THESE PIECES ASIDE.

2) USING THE 1½" STRIPS, SEW THE RIGHT SIDES TOGETHER FOR EACH OF THE FOLLOWING COMBINATIONS:
   1 BLACK STRIP TO 1 PURPLE STRIP
   1 BLACK STRIP TO 1 LIGHT YELLOW STRIP

   CUT EACH OF THESE NEWLY COMBINED STRIPS IN HALF.

IRON EACH HALF OF THE STRIPS OPEN IN OPPOSITE DIRECTIONS. FOR EXAMPLE, IRON HALF OF THE BLACK/PURPLE STRIP TOWARDS THE BLACK AND THE OTHER HALF TOWARDS THE PURPLE. THESE NEW STRIPS SHOULD NOW MEASURE 2½" IN WIDTH.

3) TAKE THE BLACK/PURPLE STRIPS AND NEST THE SEAMS (LINING THE SEAMS UP IN OPPOSITE DIRECTIONS TO ALLOW THE FABRIC TO LINE UP PERFECTLY) BY LAYING ONE RIGHT SIDE UP AND THE OTHER WRONG SIDE UP ON TOP OF IT. LINE YOUR STRIPS UP EVENLY AND TRIM THE EDGE.

TOP VIEW: SIDE VIEW:

THEN CUT (3) SETS OF 2½" X 2½" SQUARES (6 TOTAL),   (8) SETS OF 2½" X 1½" RECTANGLES (16 TOTAL)

REPEAT THIS PROCESS FOR EACH SET OF STRIPS CUTTING:

BLACK/LIGHT YELLOW - (1) SET OF 2½" X 1½" RECTANGLES (2 TOTAL)

4) NOW IT IS TIME TO LAY OUT ALL OF THE PIECES. START WITH THE FIRST ROW AND LAY EACH PIECE RIGHT SIDE UP, MAKING SURE YOU PAY ATTENTION TO THE DIRECTION THE SEAM IS FACING. ALWAYS MAKE SURE THE SEAM IS FACING THE DIRECTION OF THE ARROW. IF THE SEAM IS FACING UP OR DOWN, MAKE SURE THAT THE PIECE NEXT TO IT IS NESTED (HAS THE SEAM IN THE OPPOSITE DIRECTION). RE-IRON ANY SEAMS THAT NEED TO BE CHANGED TO A DIFFERENT DIRECTION.

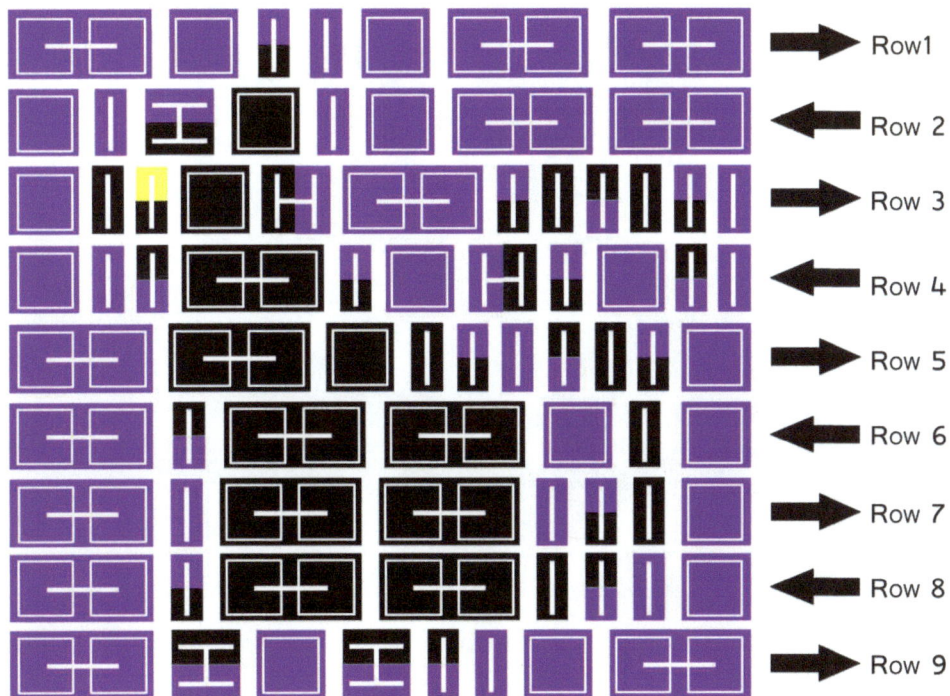

Row 1
Row 2
Row 3
Row 4
Row 5
Row 6
Row 7
Row 8
Row 9

(17)

5) ASSEMBLE EACH ROW, SEWING RIGHT SIDES TOGETHER AND SEAMS FACING THE DIRECTION OF THE ARROW.

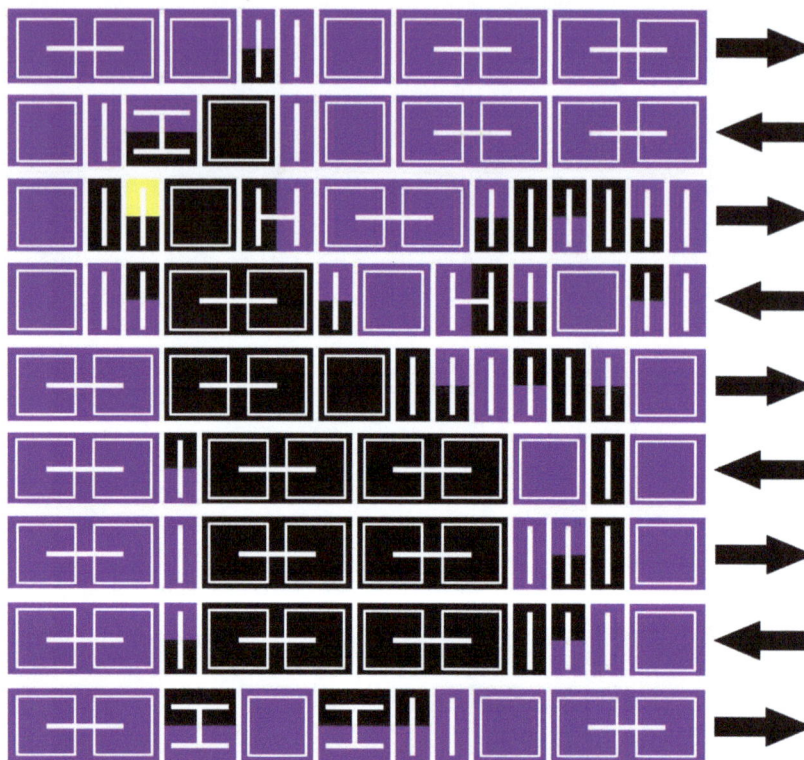

6) SEW THE ROWS TOGETHER, IT DOES NOT MATTER WHICH DIRECTION YOUR SEAMS POINT.

7) "SQUARE" YOUR BLOCK. TRIM THE EDGES OF YOUR BLOCK SO THEY ARE EVEN AND YOUR BLOCK IS 18" BY 18".

8) IF THIS BLOCK IS BEING MADE AS PART OF THE PIXELATED HALLOWEEN QUILT A LONG, SET ASIDE ANY FABRIC AND COMBINED STRIPS YOU DIDN'T USE FOR FUTURE BLOCKS.

BLOCK 6 -- CANDLE

FINISHED BLOCK MEASURES 18" BY 18".

TEXT IN A HIGHLIGHTED BLOCK INDICATES A QUILTING TIP AND CAN BE SKIPPED BY EXPERIENCED QUILTERS.

BEFORE CUTTING STRIPS OF FABRIC, MAKE SURE YOUR FABRIC IS WASHED AND IRONED. CUT STRIPS FROM SELVAGE TO SELVAGE (ALONG THE LENGTH SO STRIPS ARE ALWAYS A MINIMUM OF 40 INCHES) USING A ROTARY CUTTER AND A STRAIGHT EDGE. ALWAYS TRIM THE SELVAGE BEFORE YOU BEGIN CUTTING A NEW FABRIC AND USE A ¼ INCH SEAM WHEN SEWING TOGETHER FABRICS. THE "RIGHT" SIDE OF THE FABRIC IS THE ONE WITH THE DESIGN OR MOST COLOR. THE "WRONG" SIDE IS THE BACK OF THE FABRIC.

IF YOU ARE MAKING THIS BLOCK AS A STANDALONE AND NOT PART OF THE PIXELATED HALLOWEEN QUILT A LONG, ½ YARD OF DARK GRAY FABRIC AND ¼ YARD OF WHITE, BLACK, BROWN AND LIGHT YELLOW FABRIC ARE NEEDED.

IF THIS BLOCK IS BEING MADE AS PART OF THE PIXELATED HALLOWEEN QUILT A LONG, USE THE FOLLOWING STRIPS FROM PREVIOUS BLOCKS (AND DO NOT CUT ADDITIONAL STRIPS OF THEM, DEDUCT THIS NUMBER OF STRIPS FROM THE CHART BELOW):
(1) BLACK 2½" STRIP, (1) BROWN 2½" STRIP, (1) DARK GRAY 2½" STRIP AND (1) LIGHT YELLOW 2½" STRIP
BROWN/DARK GRAY COMBINED STRIP (DO NOT CUT 1 OF THE 1½" STRIPS OF EACH COLOR)

1) CUT THE FOLLOWING FABRICS:

COLOR		2½" STRIP	1½" STRIP
	WHITE	0	1
	BLACK	1	2
	BROWN	1	2
	DARK GRAY	4	3
	LIGHT YELLOW	1	1

FROM THE 1½" STRIPS:
CUT 1 WHITE STRIP, 1 BLACK STRIP, 1 BROWN STRIP, 1 LIGHT YELLOW AND 1 DARK GRAY STRIP IN HALF

WITH THE 2½" STRIPS:
FROM THE BLACK FABRIC CUT (1) 2½" X 1½" RECTANGLE

FROM THE DARK GRAY FABRIC CUT (18) 2½" X 4½" RECTANGLES, (12) 2½" X 2½" SQUARES,

AND (10) 2½" X 1½" RECTANGLES

FROM THE BROWN FABRIC CUT (1) 2½" X 1½" RECTANGLE

FROM THE LIGHT YELLOW FABRIC CUT (3) 2½" X 4½" RECTANGLES, (1) 2½" X 2½" SQUARE,

AND (1) 2½" X 1½" RECTANGLE

SET THESE PIECES ASIDE.

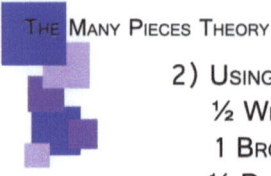

2) USING THE 1½" STRIPS, SEW THE RIGHT SIDES TOGETHER FOR EACH OF THE FOLLOWING COMBINATIONS:

½ WHITE STRIP TO ½ BLACK STRIP   1 BLACK STRIP TO 1 DARK GRAY STRIP

1 BROWN STRIP TO 1 DARK GRAY STRIP   ½ BROWN STRIP TO ½ LIGHT YELLOW STRIP

½ DARK GRAY STRIP TO ½ LIGHT YELLOW STRIP

CUT EACH OF THESE NEWLY COMBINED STRIPS IN HALF.

IRON EACH HALF OF THE STRIPS OPEN IN OPPOSITE DIRECTIONS. FOR EXAMPLE, IRON HALF OF THE BROWN/DARK GRAY STRIP TOWARDS THE BROWN AND THE OTHER HALF TOWARDS THE DARK GRAY. THESE NEW STRIPS SHOULD NOW MEASURE 2½" IN WIDTH.

3) TAKE THE BROWN/DARK GRAY STRIPS AND NEST THE SEAMS (LINING THE SEAMS UP IN OPPOSITE DIRECTIONS TO ALLOW THE FABRIC TO LINE UP PERFECTLY) BY LAYING ONE RIGHT SIDE UP AND THE OTHER WRONG SIDE UP ON TOP OF IT. LINE YOUR STRIPS UP EVENLY AND TRIM THE EDGE.

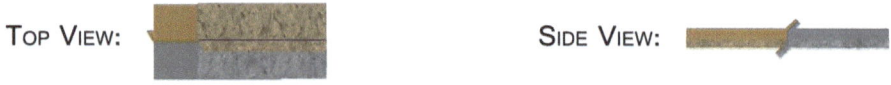

TOP VIEW: SIDE VIEW:

THEN CUT (4) SETS OF 2½" x 2½" SQUARES (8 TOTAL),   (3) SETS OF 2½" x 1½" RECTANGLES (6 TOTAL)

REPEAT THIS PROCESS FOR EACH SET OF STRIPS CUTTING:

WHITE/BLACK - (1) SET OF 2½" x 1½" RECTANGLES (2 TOTAL)

BLACK/DARK GRAY - (1) SET OF 2½" x 2½" SQUARES (2 TOTAL),   (2) SETS OF 2½" x 1½" RECTANGLES (4 TOTAL)

BROWN/LIGHT YELLOW - (2) SETS OF 2½" x 2½" SQUARES (4 TOTAL)

DARK GRAY/LIGHT YELLOW - (1) SET OF 2½" x 1½" RECTANGLES (2 TOTAL)

SET ANY EXTRA PIECES ASIDE FOR FUTURE BLOCKS.

4) NOW IT IS TIME TO LAY OUT ALL OF THE PIECES. START WITH THE FIRST ROW AND LAY EACH PIECE RIGHT SIDE UP, MAKING SURE YOU PAY ATTENTION TO THE DIRECTION THE SEAM IS FACING. ALWAYS MAKE SURE THE SEAM IS FACING THE DIRECTION OF THE ARROW. IF THE SEAM IS FACING UP OR DOWN, MAKE SURE THAT THE PIECE NEXT TO IT IS NESTED (HAS THE SEAM IN THE OPPOSITE DIRECTION). RE-IRON ANY SEAMS THAT NEED TO BE CHANGED TO A DIFFERENT DIRECTION.

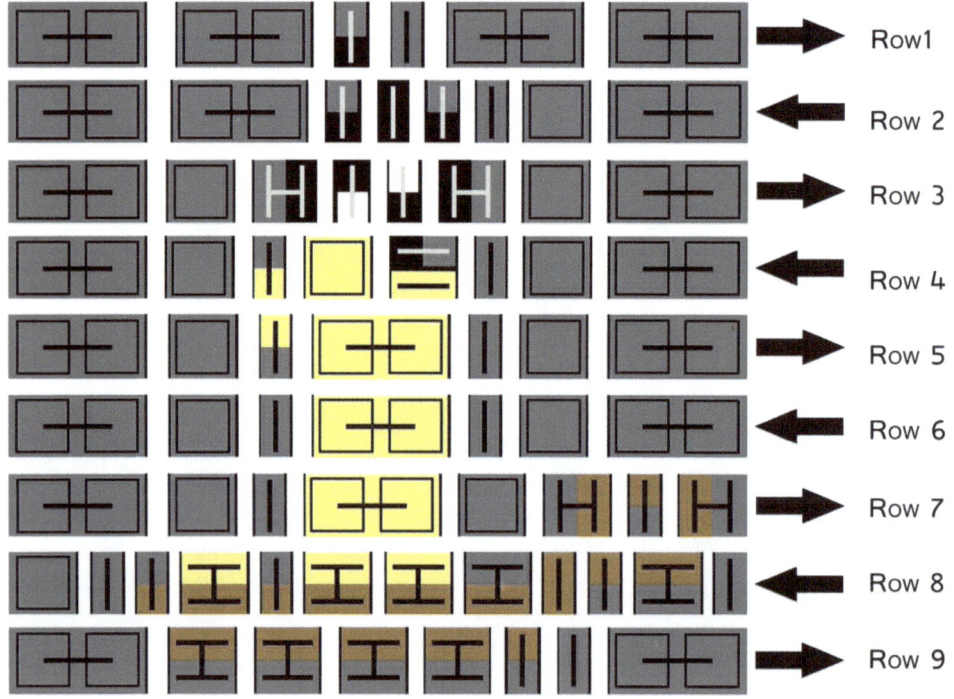

Row1

Row 2

Row 3

Row 4

Row 5

Row 6

Row 7

Row 8

Row 9

(20)

5) SEW TOGETHER THE ONE PIECE THAT NEEDS TO BE ASSEMBLED HORIZONTALLY.

Row 4

6) ASSEMBLE EACH ROW, SEWING RIGHT SIDES TOGETHER AND SEAMS FACING THE DIRECTION OF THE ARROW.

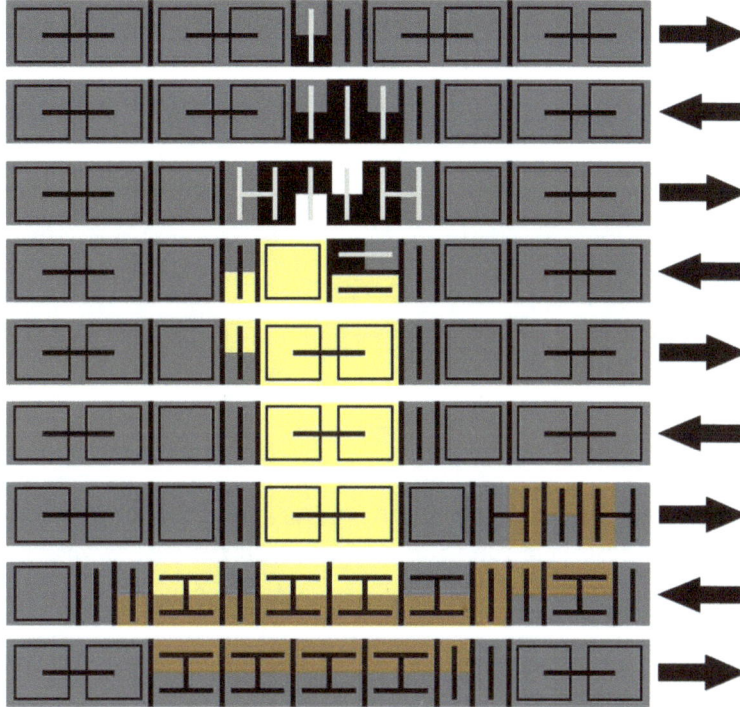

7) SEW THE ROWS TOGETHER, IT DOES NOT MATTER WHICH DIRECTION YOUR SEAMS POINT.

8) "SQUARE" YOUR BLOCK. TRIM THE EDGES OF YOUR BLOCK SO THEY ARE EVEN AND YOUR BLOCK IS 18" BY 18".

9) IF THIS BLOCK IS BEING MADE AS PART OF THE PIXELATED HALLOWEEN QUILT A LONG, SET ASIDE ANY FABRIC AND COMBINED STRIPS YOU DIDN'T USE FOR FUTURE BLOCKS.

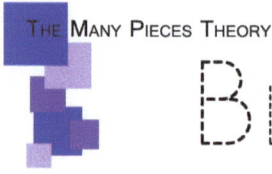

BLOCK 7 - GHOST

FINISHED BLOCK MEASURES 18" BY 18".

BEFORE CUTTING STRIPS OF FABRIC, MAKE SURE YOUR FABRIC IS WASHED AND IRONED. CUT STRIPS FROM SELVAGE TO SELVAGE (ALONG THE LENGTH SO STRIPS ARE ALWAYS A MINIMUM OF 40 INCHES) USING A ROTARY CUTTER AND A STRAIGHT EDGE. ALWAYS TRIM THE SELVAGE BEFORE YOU BEGIN CUTTING A NEW FABRIC AND USE A ¼ INCH SEAM WHEN SEWING TOGETHER FABRICS. THE "RIGHT" SIDE OF THE FABRIC IS THE ONE WITH THE DESIGN OR MOST COLOR. THE "WRONG" SIDE IS THE BACK OF THE FABRIC.

IF YOU ARE MAKING THIS BLOCK AS A STANDALONE AND NOT PART OF THE PIXELATED HALLOWEEN QUILT A LONG, ¼ YARD OF DARK GRAY, WHITE AND BLACK FABRIC ARE NEEDED.

IF THIS BLOCK IS BEING MADE AS PART OF THE PIXELATED HALLOWEEN QUILT A LONG, USE THE FOLLOWING STRIPS FROM PREVIOUS BLOCKS (AND DO NOT CUT ADDITIONAL STRIPS OF THEM, DEDUCT THIS NUMBER OF STRIPS FROM THE CHART BELOW): (1) BLACK 2 ½" STRIP, WHITE/BLACK COMBINED STRIP (DO NOT CUT 1 OF THE 1 ½" STRIPS OF EACH COLOR)

1) CUT THE FOLLOWING FABRICS:

COLOR		2½" STRIP	1½" STRIP
	WHITE	2	2
	BLACK	1	2
	DARK GRAY	2	2

SET ASIDE THE 1½" STRIPS.

WITH THE 2 ½" STRIPS:
FROM THE BLACK FABRIC CUT (2) 2 ½ " X 1 ½" RECTANGLES

FROM THE DARK GRAY FABRIC CUT (7) 2½" X 4½" RECTANGLES, (10) 2½" X 2½" SQUARES, AND (11) 2½" X 1½" RECTANGLES

FROM THE WHITE FABRIC CUT (10) 2 ½ " X 4 ½" RECTANGLES, (7) 2 ½" X 2 ½" SQUARES, AND (2) 2 ½ " X 1 ½" RECTANGLES

SET THESE PIECES ASIDE.

2) USING THE 1½" STRIPS, SEW THE RIGHT SIDES TOGETHER FOR EACH OF THE FOLLOWING COMBINATIONS:

1 WHITE STRIP TO 1 BLACK STRIP   1 WHITE STRIP TO 1 DARK GRAY STRIP

1 BLACK STRIP TO 1 DARK GRAY STRIP

CUT EACH OF THESE NEWLY COMBINED STRIPS IN HALF.

IRON EACH HALF OF THE STRIPS OPEN IN OPPOSITE DIRECTIONS. FOR EXAMPLE, IRON HALF OF THE WHITE/DARK GRAY STRIP TOWARDS THE WHITE AND THE OTHER HALF TOWARDS THE DARK GRAY. THESE NEW STRIPS SHOULD NOW MEASURE 2½" IN WIDTH.

3) TAKE THE WHITE/DARK GRAY STRIPS AND NEST THE SEAMS (LINING THE SEAMS UP IN OPPOSITE DIRECTIONS TO ALLOW THE FABRIC TO LINE UP PERFECTLY) BY LAYING ONE RIGHT SIDE UP AND THE OTHER WRONG SIDE UP ON TOP OF IT. LINE YOUR STRIPS UP EVENLY AND TRIM THE EDGE.

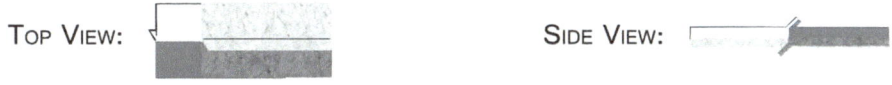

TOP VIEW: SIDE VIEW:

THEN CUT (3) SETS OF 2½" X 2½" SQUARES (6 TOTAL), (3) SETS OF 2½" X 1½" RECTANGLES (6 TOTAL)

REPEAT THIS PROCESS FOR EACH SET OF STRIPS CUTTING:

WHITE/BLACK - (3) SETS OF 2½" X 1½" RECTANGLES (6 TOTAL)

BLACK/DARK GRAY - (5) SETS OF 2½" X 2½" SQUARES (10 TOTAL),

(4) SETS OF 2½" X 1½" RECTANGLES (8 TOTAL)

SET ANY EXTRA PIECES ASIDE FOR FUTURE BLOCKS.

4) NOW IT IS TIME TO LAY OUT ALL OF THE PIECES. START WITH THE FIRST ROW AND LAY EACH PIECE RIGHT SIDE UP, MAKING SURE YOU PAY ATTENTION TO THE DIRECTION THE SEAM IS FACING. ALWAYS MAKE SURE THE SEAM IS FACING THE DIRECTION OF THE ARROW. IF THE SEAM IS FACING UP OR DOWN, MAKE SURE THAT THE PIECE NEXT TO IT IS NESTED (HAS THE SEAM IN THE OPPOSITE DIRECTION). RE-IRON ANY SEAMS THAT NEED TO BE CHANGED TO A DIFFERENT DIRECTION.

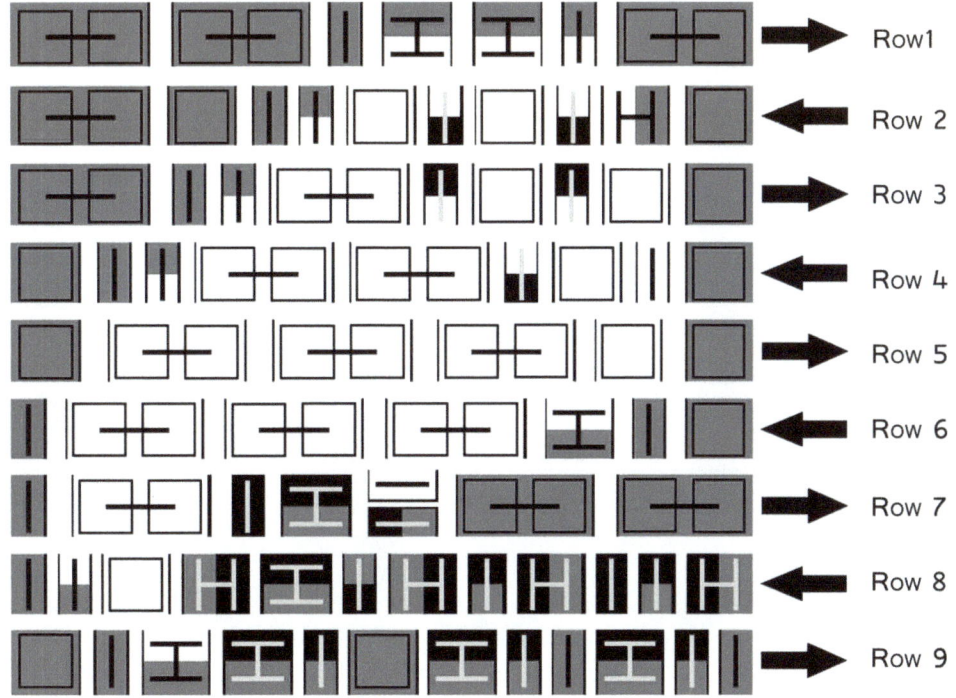

Row 1

Row 2

Row 3

Row 4

Row 5

Row 6

Row 7

Row 8

Row 9

(23)

5) Sew together the one piece that needs to be assembled horizontally.

Row 7

6) Assemble each row, sewing right sides together and seams facing the direction of the arrow.

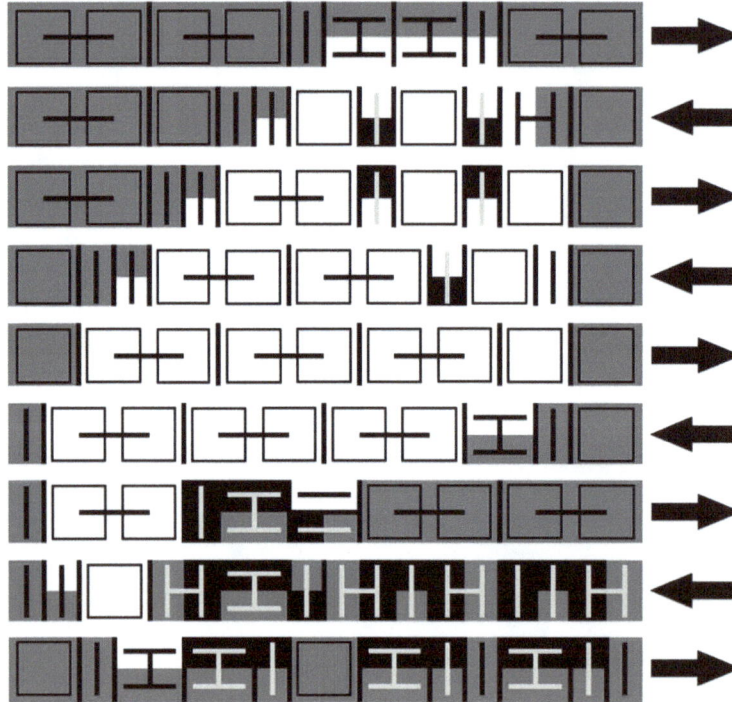

7) Sew the rows together, it does not matter which direction your seams point.

8) "Square" your block. Trim the edges of your block so they are even and your block is 18" by 18".

9) If this block is being made as part of the Pixelated Halloween Quilt a Long, set aside any fabric and combined strips you didn't use for future blocks.

Block 8
– Poison

Finished block measures 18" by 18".

Before cutting strips of fabric, make sure your fabric is washed and ironed. Cut strips from selvage to selvage (along the length so strips are always a minimum of 40 inches) using a rotary cutter and a straight edge. Always trim the selvage before you begin cutting a new fabric and use a ¼ inch seam when sewing together fabrics. The "right" side of the fabric is the one with the design or most color. The "wrong" side is the back of the fabric.

If you are making this block as a standalone and not part of the Pixelated Halloween Quilt a Long, ½ yard of Apple Green fabric and ¼ yard of Brown, Light Blue, Purple and White fabric are needed.

If this block is being made as part of the Pixelated Halloween Quilt a Long, use the following strips from previous blocks (and do not cut additional strips of them, deduct this number of strips from the chart below):
1 Apple Green 2 ½" strip,   Brown 2 ½" Strip,   Light Blue 2 ½" Strip,   White 2 ½" Strip,
½ Brown 1 ½" Strip (do not cut the 1 ½" strip)

1) Cut the Following Fabrics:

Color		2½" Strip	1½" Strip
	Apple Green	3	2
	Brown	1	1
	Light Blue	1	2
	Purple	1	2
	White	1	1

From the 1 ½ " strips:
Cut 1 Apple Green strip and the Brown strip in half (If you pulled the ½ Brown strip do NOT cut in half)
With the 2½" strips:
From the Apple Green fabric cut (14) 2½" x 4½" rectangles,   (8) 2½" x 2½" squares,

and (8) 2½" x 1½" rectangles
From the White fabric cut (1) 2½" x 2½" square   and (4) 2½" x 1½" rectangles

From the Light Blue fabric cut (2) 2½" x 1½" rectangles

From the Purple fabric cut (1) 2½" x 4½" rectangle,   (2) 2½" x 2½" squares,

and (4) 2½" x 1½" rectangles
From the Brown fabric cut (1) 2½" x 4½" rectangle   and (1) 2½" x 2½" square
Set these pieces aside.

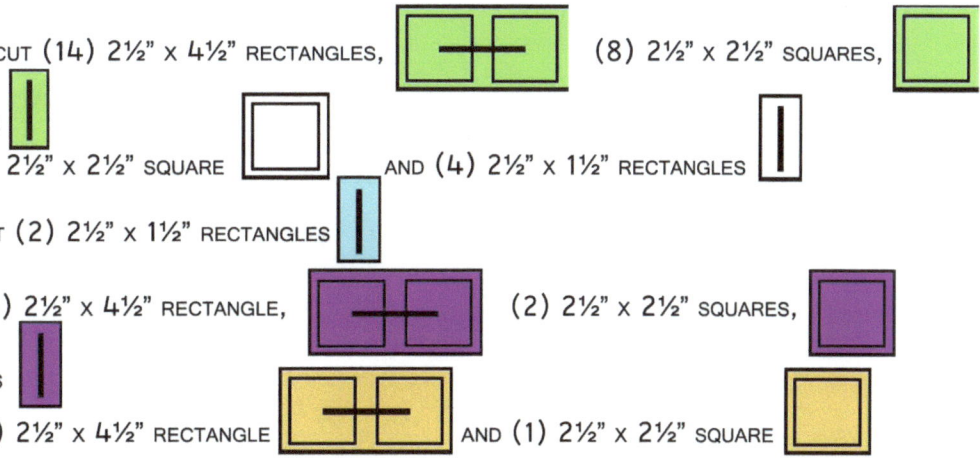

2) Using the 1½" strips, sew the right sides together for each of the following combinations:

½ Apple Green Strip to ½ Brown Strip   1 Apple Green Strip to 1 Light Blue Strip

1 Light Blue Strip to 1 Purple Strip   1 Purple Strip to 1 White Strip

Cut each of these newly combined strips in half.

Iron each half of the strips open in opposite directions. For example, iron half of the Apple Green/Light Blue strip towards the Apple Green and the other half towards the Light Blue. These new strips should now measure 2½" in width.

3) Take the Apple Green/Light Blue strips and nest the seams (lining the seams up in opposite directions to allow the fabric to line up perfectly) by laying one right side up and the other wrong side up on top of it. Line your strips up evenly and trim the edge.

Top View: Side View:

Then cut (3) sets of 2½" x 2½" squares (6 total),   (5) sets of 2½" x 1½" rectangles (10 total)

Repeat this process for each set of strips cutting:

Apple Green/Brown - (2) sets of 2½" x 2½" squares (4 total)

Light Blue/Purple - (3) sets of 2½" x 2½" squares (6 total),   (2) sets of 2½" x 1½" rectangles (4 total)

Purple/White - (3) sets of 2½" x 2½" squares (6 total),   (2) sets of 2½" x 1½" rectangles (4 total)

Set any extra pieces aside for future blocks.

4) Now it is time to lay out all of the pieces. Start with the first row and lay each piece right side up, making sure you pay attention to the direction the seam is facing. Always make sure the seam is facing the direction of the arrow. If the seam is facing up or down, make sure that the piece next to it is nested (has the seam in the opposite direction). Re-iron any seams that need to be changed to a different direction.

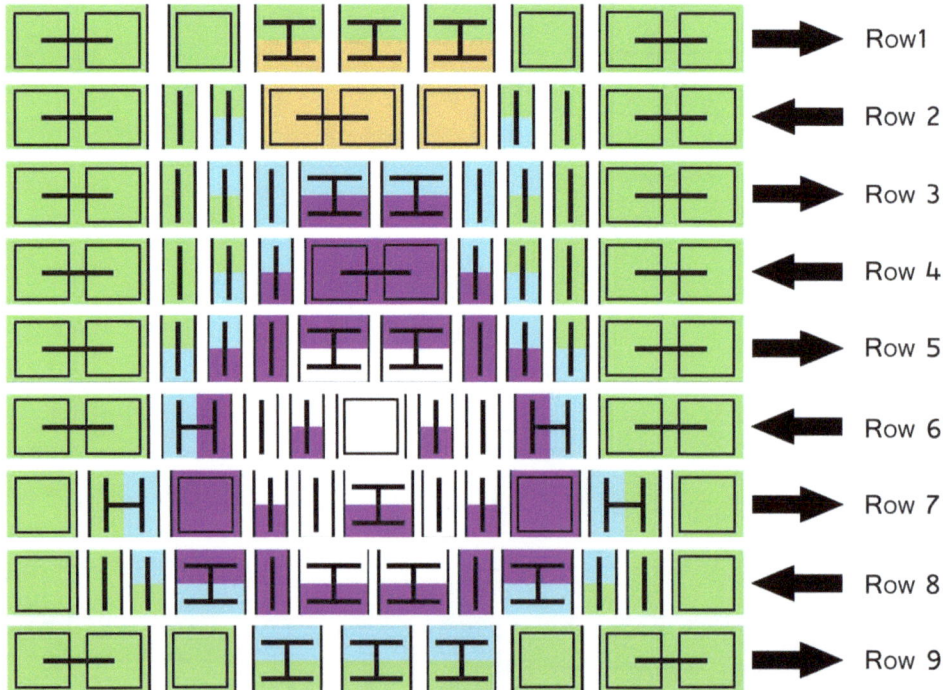

Row 1
Row 2
Row 3
Row 4
Row 5
Row 6
Row 7
Row 8
Row 9

5) Assemble each row, sewing right sides together and seams facing the direction of the arrow.

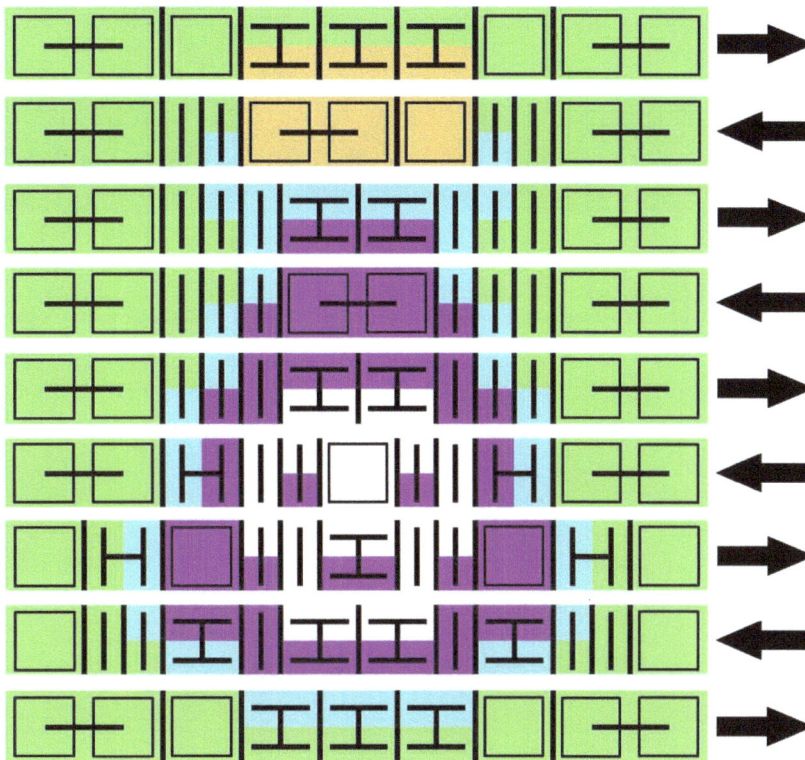

6) Sew the rows together, it does not matter which direction your seams point.

7) "Square" your block. Trim the edges of your block so they are even and your block is 18" by 18".

8) If this block is being made as part of the Pixelated Halloween Quilt a Long, set aside any fabric and combined strips you didn't use for future blocks.

BLOCK 9
- MAGIC

FINISHED BLOCK MEASURES 18" BY 18".

TEXT IN A HIGHLIGHTED BLOCK INDICATES A QUILTING TIP AND CAN BE SKIPPED BY EXPERIENCED QUILTERS.

BEFORE CUTTING STRIPS OF FABRIC, MAKE SURE YOUR FABRIC IS WASHED AND IRONED. CUT STRIPS FROM SELVAGE TO SELVAGE (ALONG THE LENGTH SO STRIPS ARE ALWAYS A MINIMUM OF 40 INCHES) USING A ROTARY CUTTER AND A STRAIGHT EDGE. ALWAYS TRIM THE SELVAGE BEFORE YOU BEGIN CUTTING A NEW FABRIC AND USE A ¼ INCH SEAM WHEN SEWING TOGETHER FABRICS. THE "RIGHT" SIDE OF THE FABRIC IS THE ONE WITH THE DESIGN OR MOST COLOR. THE "WRONG" SIDE IS THE BACK OF THE FABRIC.

IF YOU ARE MAKING THIS BLOCK AS A STANDALONE AND NOT PART OF THE PIXELATED HALLOWEEN QUILT A LONG, ½ YARD OF DARK BLUE FABRIC AND ¼ YARD OF LIGHT BLUE AND PURPLE FABRIC ARE NEEDED.

IF THIS BLOCK IS BEING MADE AS PART OF THE PIXELATED HALLOWEEN QUILT A LONG, USE THE FOLLOWING STRIPS FROM PREVIOUS BLOCKS (AND DO NOT CUT ADDITIONAL STRIPS OF THEM, DEDUCT THIS NUMBER OF STRIPS FROM THE CHART BELOW):

PURPLE 2½" STRIP   LIGHT BLUE 2½" STRIP

1) CUT THE FOLLOWING FABRICS:

	COLOR	2½" STRIP	1½" STRIP
	LIGHT BLUE	1	1
	PURPLE	1	2
	DARK BLUE	3	3

WITH THE 2 ½" STRIPS:

FROM THE LIGHT BLUE FABRIC CUT (2) 2½" X 1½" RECTANGLES

FROM THE PURPLE FABRIC CUT (3) 2½ " X 1½" RECTANGLES

FROM THE DARK BLUE FABRIC CUT (15) 2½" X 4½" RECTANGLES,   (14) 2½" X 2½" SQUARES,

AND (10) 2½ " X 1½" RECTANGLES

SET THESE PIECES ASIDE.

2) USING THE 1½" STRIPS, SEW THE RIGHT SIDES TOGETHER FOR EACH OF THE FOLLOWING COMBINATIONS:

    1 LIGHT BLUE STRIP TO 1 DARK BLUE STRIP

    2 PURPLE STRIPS TO 2 DARK BLUE STRIPS

CUT EACH OF THESE NEWLY COMBINED STRIPS IN HALF.

IRON EACH HALF OF THE STRIPS OPEN IN OPPOSITE DIRECTIONS. FOR EXAMPLE, IRON HALF OF THE LIGHT BLUE/DARK BLUE STRIP TOWARDS THE LIGHT BLUE AND THE OTHER HALF TOWARDS THE DARK BLUE. THESE NEW STRIPS SHOULD NOW MEASURE 2½" IN WIDTH.

3) TAKE THE LIGHT BLUE/DARK BLUE STRIPS AND NEST THE SEAMS (LINING THE SEAMS UP IN OPPOSITE DIRECTIONS TO ALLOW THE FABRIC TO LINE UP PERFECTLY) BY LAYING ONE RIGHT SIDE UP AND THE OTHER WRONG SIDE UP ON TOP OF IT. LINE YOUR STRIPS UP EVENLY AND TRIM THE EDGE.

TOP VIEW: SIDE VIEW:

THEN CUT (3) SETS OF 2½" x 2½" SQUARES (6 TOTAL),   (4) SETS OF 2½" x 1½" RECTANGLES (8 TOTAL)

REPEAT THIS PROCESS FOR EACH SET OF STRIPS CUTTING:

PURPLE/DARK BLUE - (6) SETS OF 2½" x 2½" SQUARES (12 TOTAL),

(9) SETS OF 2½" x 1½" RECTANGLES (18 TOTAL)

4) NOW IT IS TIME TO LAY OUT ALL OF THE PIECES. START WITH THE FIRST ROW AND LAY EACH PIECE RIGHT SIDE UP, MAKING SURE YOU PAY ATTENTION TO THE DIRECTION THE SEAM IS FACING. ALWAYS MAKE SURE THE SEAM IS FACING THE DIRECTION OF THE ARROW. IF THE SEAM IS FACING UP OR DOWN, MAKE SURE THAT THE PIECE NEXT TO IT IS NESTED (HAS THE SEAM IN THE OPPOSITE DIRECTION). RE-IRON ANY SEAMS THAT NEED TO BE CHANGED TO A DIFFERENT DIRECTION.

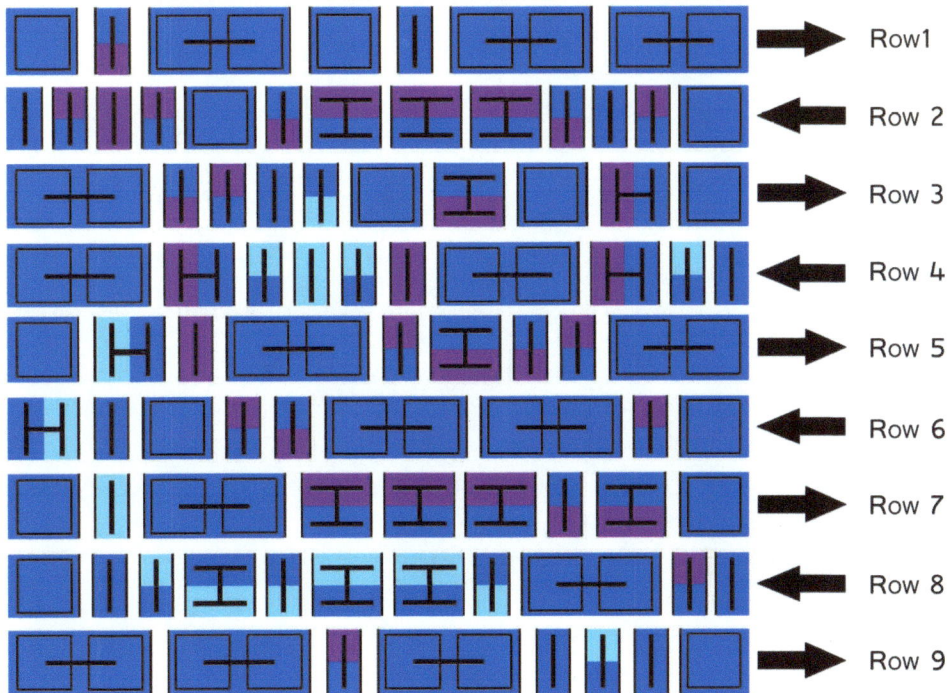

Row 1

Row 2

Row 3

Row 4

Row 5

Row 6

Row 7

Row 8

Row 9

(29)

5) Assemble each row, sewing right sides together and seams facing the direction of the arrow.

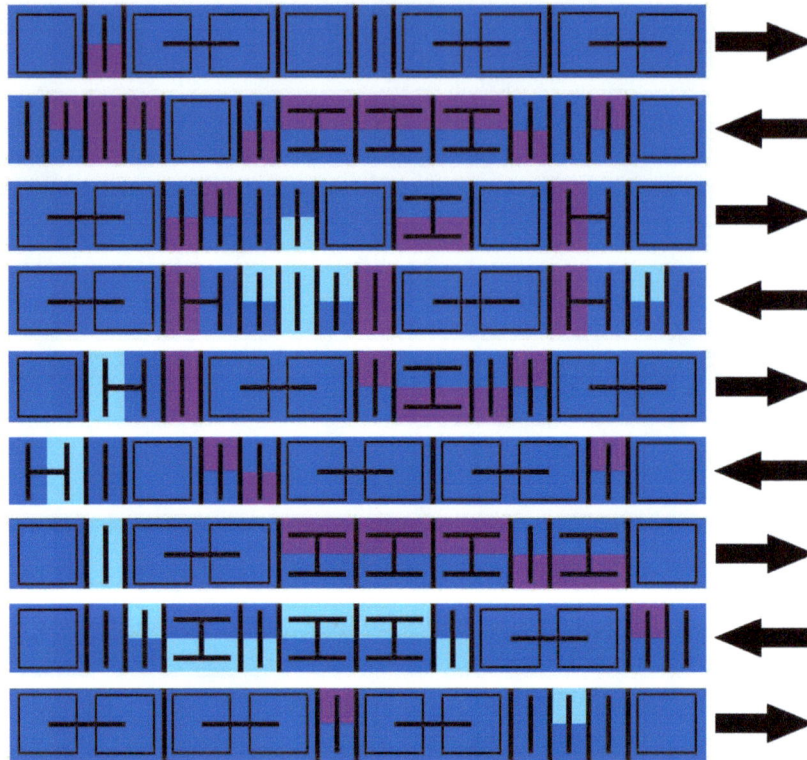

6) Sew the rows together, it does not matter which direction your seams point.

7) "Square" your block. Trim the edges of your block so they are even and your block is 18" by 18".

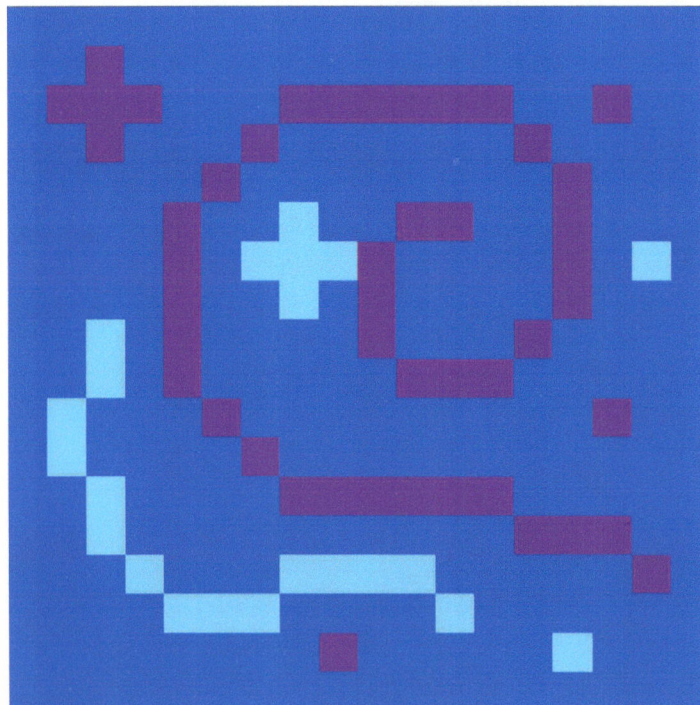

8) If this block is being made as part of the Pixelated Halloween Quilt a Long, set aside any fabric and combined strips you didn't use for future blocks.

BLOCK 10
- HAT

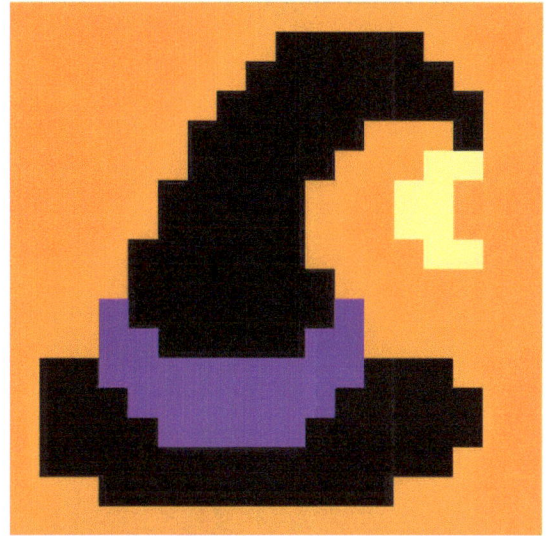

FINISHED BLOCK MEASURES 18" BY 18".

TEXT IN A HIGHLIGHTED BLOCK INDICATES A QUILTING TIP AND CAN BE SKIPPED BY EXPERIENCED QUILTERS.

BEFORE CUTTING STRIPS OF FABRIC, MAKE SURE YOUR FABRIC IS WASHED AND IRONED. CUT STRIPS FROM SELVAGE TO SELVAGE (ALONG THE LENGTH SO STRIPS ARE ALWAYS A MINIMUM OF 40 INCHES) USING A ROTARY CUTTER AND A STRAIGHT EDGE. ALWAYS TRIM THE SELVAGE BEFORE YOU BEGIN CUTTING A NEW FABRIC AND USE A ¼ INCH SEAM WHEN SEWING TOGETHER FABRICS. THE "RIGHT" SIDE OF THE FABRIC IS THE ONE WITH THE DESIGN OR MOST COLOR. THE "WRONG" SIDE IS THE BACK OF THE FABRIC.

IF YOU ARE MAKING THIS BLOCK AS A STANDALONE AND NOT PART OF THE PIXELATED HALLOWEEN QUILT A LONG, ½ YARD OF ORANGE AND ¼ YARD OF BLACK, PURPLE AND LIGHT YELLOW FABRIC ARE NEEDED.

IF THIS BLOCK IS BEING MADE AS PART OF THE PIXELATED HALLOWEEN QUILT A LONG, USE THE FOLLOWING STRIPS FROM PREVIOUS BLOCKS (AND DO NOT CUT ADDITIONAL STRIPS OF THEM, DEDUCT THIS NUMBER OF STRIPS FROM THE CHART BELOW):

1 BLACK 2 ½" STRIP   THE PURPLE 2 ½" STRIP   1 ORANGE 2 ½" STRIP   THE LIGHT YELLOW 2 ½" STRIP

½ BLACK 1 ½" STRIP (DO NOT CUT 1 OF THE 1 ½" STRIPS)

ORANGE/LIGHT YELLOW COMBINED STRIP (DO NOT CUT 1 OF THE 1 ½" STRIPS OF EACH COLOR)

1) CUT THE FOLLOWING FABRICS:

	COLOR	2½" STRIP	1½" STRIP
⬛	BLACK	2	2
🟪	PURPLE	1	1
🟧	ORANGE	3	2
🟨	LIGHT YELLOW	1	1

FROM THE 1 ½ " STRIPS:

CUT 1 BLACK STRIP (IF YOU PULLED FROM PREVIOUS BLOCKS DO NOT CUT IN HALF) AND 1 PURPLE STRIP IN HALF

WITH THE 2 ½" STRIPS:

FROM THE BLACK FABRIC CUT (7) 2½ " X 4½" RECTANGLES,   (4) 2½" X 2½" SQUARES,

AND (5) 2½ " X 1½" RECTANGLES

FROM THE PURPLE FABRIC CUT (1) 2½ " X 4½" RECTANGLE,   (1) 2½" X 2½" SQUARE,

AND (3) 2½" X 1½" RECTANGLES

FROM THE ORANGE FABRIC CUT (9) 2½ " X 4½" RECTANGLES,   (14) 2½" X 2½" SQUARES,

AND (10) 2½" X 1½" RECTANGLES

FROM THE LIGHT YELLOW FABRIC CUT (1) 2½" X 2½" SQUARE   AND (1) 2½ " X 1½" RECTANGLE

SET THESE PIECES ASIDE.

(31)

2) Using the 1½" strips, sew the right sides together for each of the following combinations:

½ Black Strip to ½ Purple Strip   1 Black Strip to 1 Orange Strip

1 Orange Strip to 1 Light Yellow Strip

Cut each of these newly combined strips in half.

Iron each half of the strips open in opposite directions. For example, iron half of the Black/Purple strip towards the Black and the other half towards the Purple. These new strips should now measure 2½" in width.

3) Take the Black/Purple strips and nest the seams (lining the seams up in opposite directions to allow the fabric to line up perfectly) by laying one right side up and the other wrong side up on top of it. Line your strips up evenly and trim the edge.

Top View: Side View:

Then cut (1) set of 2½" x 2½" squares (2 total),   (3) sets of 2½" x 1½" rectangles (6 total)

Repeat this process for each set of strips cutting:

Black/Orange - (4) sets of 2½" x 2½" squares (8 total),   (4) sets of 2½" x 1½" rectangles (8 total)

Orange/Light Yellow - (1) set of 2½" x 2½" squares (2 total)

Set any extra pieces aside for future blocks.

4) Now it is time to lay out all of the pieces. Start with the first row and lay each piece right side up, making sure you pay attention to the direction the seam is facing. Always make sure the seam is facing the direction of the arrow. If the seam is facing up or down, make sure that the piece next to it is nested (has the seam in the opposite direction). Re-iron any seams that need to be changed to a different direction.

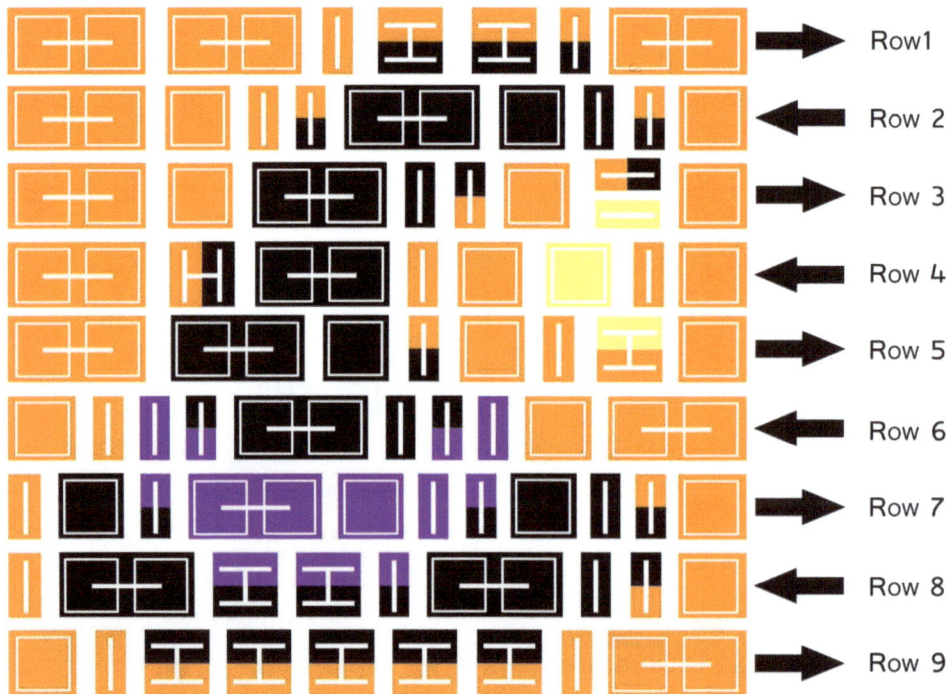

Row 1
Row 2
Row 3
Row 4
Row 5
Row 6
Row 7
Row 8
Row 9

5) SEW TOGETHER THE ONE PIECE THAT NEED TO BE ASSEMBLED HORIZONTALLY.

Row 3

6) ASSEMBLE EACH ROW, SEWING RIGHT SIDES TOGETHER AND SEAMS FACING THE DIRECTION OF THE ARROW.

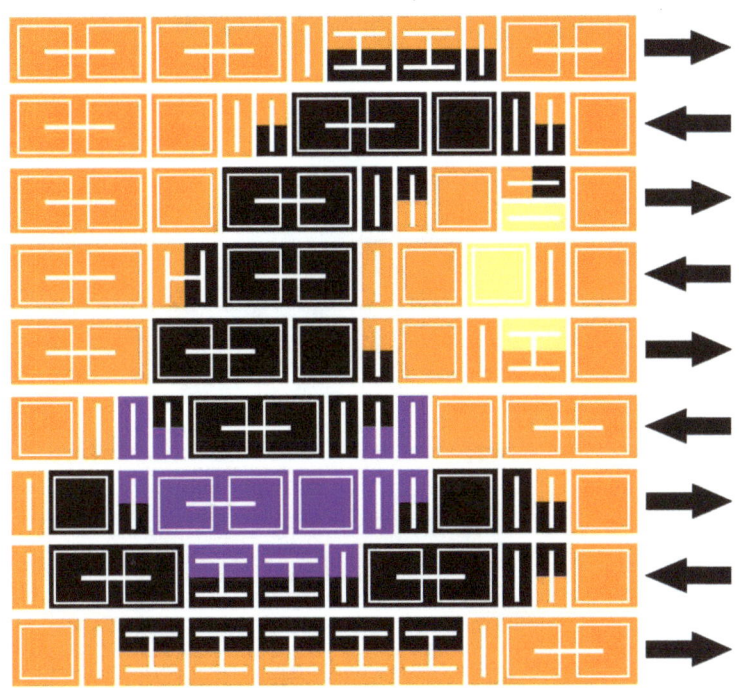

7) SEW THE ROWS TOGETHER, IT DOES NOT MATTER WHICH DIRECTION YOUR SEAMS POINT.

8) "SQUARE" YOUR BLOCK. TRIM THE EDGES OF YOUR BLOCK SO THEY ARE EVEN AND YOUR BLOCK IS 18" BY 18".

9) IF THIS BLOCK IS BEING MADE AS PART OF THE PIXELATED HALLOWEEN QUILT A LONG, SET ASIDE ANY FABRIC AND COMBINED STRIPS YOU DIDN'T USE FOR FUTURE BLOCKS.

Block 11 - Spider

Finished block measures 18" by 18".

If you are making this block as a standalone and not part of the Pixelated Halloween Quilt a Long, ½ yard of Light Yellow and ¼ yard of Black, Purple and Orange fabric are needed.

If this block is being made as part of the Pixelated Halloween Quilt a Long, use the following strips from previous blocks (and do not cut additional strips of them, deduct this number of strips from the chart below):

(1)Purple 2½" strip (½)Purple 1½" Strip (do not cut 1 of the 1½" strips)

(½)Light Yellow 1½" Strip (don't deduct strips with this one)

Black/Purple combined strip (don't deduct strips with this one)

Black/Orange combined strip (do not cut 1 of the 1½" strips of each color)

Black/Light Yellow combined strip (do not cut 1 of the 1½" strips of each color)

1) Cut the Following Fabrics:

	Color	2½" Strip	1½" Strip
⬛	Black	1	2
🟪	Purple	1	2
🟧	Orange	0	1
🟨	Light Yellow	3	2

From the 1 ½ " strips:

Cut both Black strips (if you pulled from previous blocks do not cut in half), 1 Purple strip in half (if you pulled from previous blocks do not cut in half), 1 Orange strip in half (if you pulled from previous blocks do not cut in half), 1 Light Yellow strip in half (if you pulled from previous blocks do not cut in half)

With the 2 ½" strips:
From the Black fabric cut (7) 2½" x 4½" rectangles, and (2) 2½" x 2½" squares,

From the Purple fabric cut (2) 2½ " x 1½" rectangles

From the Light Yellow fabric cut (9) 2½" x 4½" rectangles, (13) 2½" x 2½" squares,

and (14) 2½" x 1½" rectangles

Set these pieces aside.

(34)

2) USING THE 1½" STRIPS, SEW THE RIGHT SIDES TOGETHER FOR EACH OF THE FOLLOWING COMBINATIONS:

½ BLACK STRIP TO ½ PURPLE STRIP   ½ BLACK STRIP TO ½ ORANGE STRIP
½ BLACK STRIP TO ½ LIGHT YELLOW STRIP   1½ PURPLE STRIPS TO 1½ LIGHT YELLOW STRIPS

CUT EACH OF THESE NEWLY COMBINED STRIPS IN HALF.

IRON EACH HALF OF THE STRIPS OPEN IN OPPOSITE DIRECTIONS. FOR EXAMPLE, IRON HALF OF THE PURPLE/LIGHT YELLOW STRIP TOWARDS THE PURPLE AND THE OTHER HALF TOWARDS THE LIGHT YELLOW. THESE NEW STRIPS SHOULD NOW MEASURE 2½" IN WIDTH.

3) TAKE THE PURPLE/LIGHT YELLOW STRIPS AND NEST THE SEAMS (LINING THE SEAMS UP IN OPPOSITE DIRECTIONS TO ALLOW THE FABRIC TO LINE UP PERFECTLY) BY LAYING ONE RIGHT SIDE UP AND THE OTHER WRONG SIDE UP ON TOP OF IT. LINE YOUR STRIPS UP EVENLY AND TRIM THE EDGE.

TOP VIEW: SIDE VIEW:

THEN CUT (7) SETS OF 2½" X 2½" SQUARES (14 TOTAL),   (8) SETS OF 2½" X 1½" RECTANGLES (16 TOTAL)

REPEAT THIS PROCESS FOR EACH SET OF STRIPS CUTTING:

BLACK/PURPLE - (1) SET OF 2 ½" X 1 ½" RECTANGLES (2 TOTAL)

BLACK/ORANGE - (1) SET OF 2 ½" X 1 ½" RECTANGLES (2 TOTAL)

BLACK/LIGHT YELLOW - (2) SETS OF 2 ½" X 1 ½" RECTANGLES (4 TOTAL)

SET ANY EXTRA PIECES ASIDE FOR FUTURE BLOCKS.

4) NOW IT IS TIME TO LAY OUT ALL OF THE PIECES. START WITH THE FIRST ROW AND LAY EACH PIECE RIGHT SIDE UP, MAKING SURE YOU PAY ATTENTION TO THE DIRECTION THE SEAM IS FACING. ALWAYS MAKE SURE THE SEAM IS FACING THE DIRECTION OF THE ARROW. IF THE SEAM IS FACING UP OR DOWN, MAKE SURE THAT THE PIECE NEXT TO IT IS NESTED (HAS THE SEAM IN THE OPPOSITE DIRECTION). RE-IRON ANY SEAMS THAT NEED TO BE CHANGED TO A DIFFERENT DIRECTION.

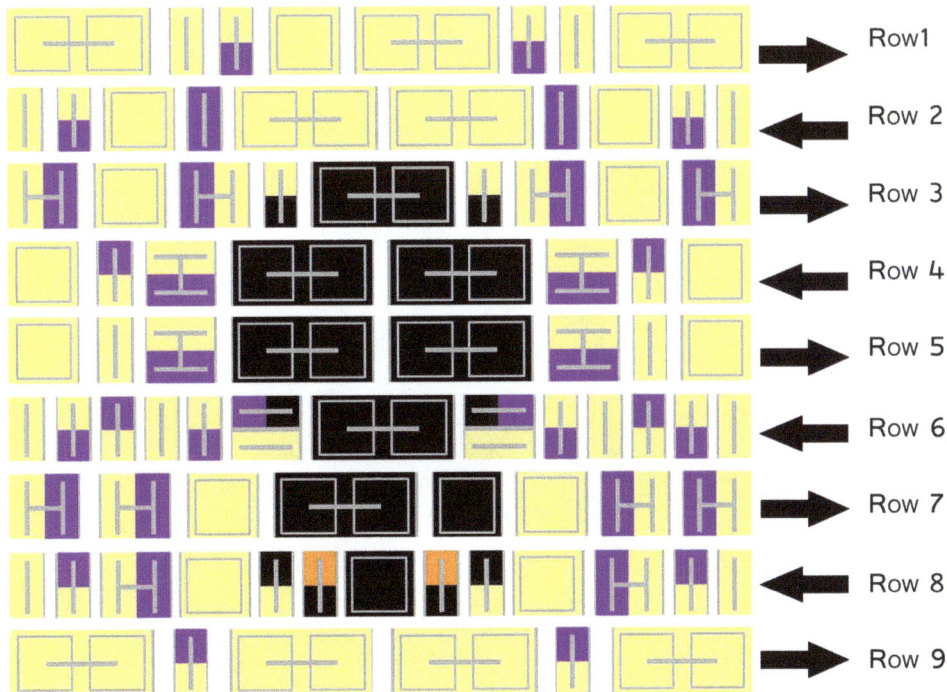

Row1
Row 2
Row 3
Row 4
Row 5
Row 6
Row 7
Row 8
Row 9

5) SEW TOGETHER THE TWO PIECES THAT NEED TO BE ASSEMBLED HORIZONTALLY.

Row 6

6) ASSEMBLE EACH ROW, SEWING RIGHT SIDES TOGETHER AND SEAMS FACING THE DIRECTION OF THE ARROW.

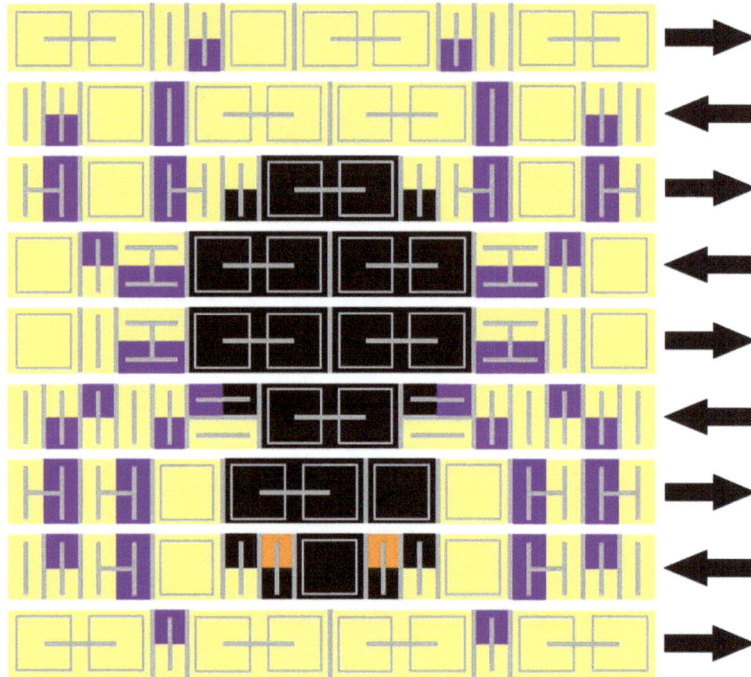

7) SEW THE ROWS TOGETHER, IT DOES NOT MATTER WHICH DIRECTION YOUR SEAMS POINT.

8) "SQUARE" YOUR BLOCK. TRIM THE EDGES OF YOUR BLOCK SO THEY ARE EVEN AND YOUR BLOCK IS 18" BY 18".

9) IF THIS BLOCK IS BEING MADE AS PART OF THE PIXELATED HALLOWEEN QUILT A LONG, SET ASIDE ANY FABRIC AND COMBINED STRIPS YOU DIDN'T USE FOR FUTURE BLOCKS.

BLOCK 12 – TOMBSTONE

FINISHED BLOCK MEASURES 18" BY 18".

TEXT IN A HIGHLIGHTED BLOCK INDICATES A QUILTING TIP AND CAN BE SKIPPED BY EXPERIENCED QUILTERS.

BEFORE CUTTING STRIPS OF FABRIC, MAKE SURE YOUR FABRIC IS WASHED AND IRONED. CUT STRIPS FROM SELVAGE TO SELVAGE (ALONG THE LENGTH SO STRIPS ARE ALWAYS A MINIMUM OF 40 INCHES) USING A ROTARY CUTTER AND A STRAIGHT EDGE. ALWAYS TRIM THE SELVAGE BEFORE YOU BEGIN CUTTING A NEW FABRIC AND USE A ¼ INCH SEAM WHEN SEWING TOGETHER FABRICS. THE "RIGHT" SIDE OF THE FABRIC IS THE ONE WITH THE DESIGN OR MOST COLOR. THE "WRONG" SIDE IS THE BACK OF THE FABRIC.

IF YOU ARE MAKING THIS BLOCK AS A STANDALONE AND NOT PART OF THE PIXELATED HALLOWEEN QUILT A LONG, ¼ YARD OF BROWN, DARK GRAY AND LIGHT GRAY FABRIC ARE NEEDED.

IF THIS BLOCK IS BEING MADE AS PART OF THE PIXELATED HALLOWEEN QUILT A LONG, USE THE FOLLOWING STRIPS FROM PREVIOUS BLOCKS (AND DO NOT CUT ADDITIONAL STRIPS OF THEM, DEDUCT THIS NUMBER OF STRIPS FROM THE CHART BELOW):

DARK GRAY 2½" STRIP   (1) LIGHT GRAY 2½" STRIP

1) CUT THE FOLLOWING FABRICS:

COLOR		2½" STRIP	1½" STRIP
	BROWN	2	2
	DARK GRAY	1	3
	LIGHT GRAY	2	1

SET ASIDE THE 1 ½ " STRIPS.

WITH THE 2 ½" STRIPS:

FROM THE BROWN FABRIC CUT (5) 2½ " X 4½" RECTANGLES, (13) 2½" X 2½" SQUARES,

AND (5) 2½ " X 1½" RECTANGLES

FROM THE DARK GRAY FABRIC CUT (2) 2½ " X 1½" RECTANGLES

FROM THE LIGHT GRAY FABRIC CUT (8) 2½" X 4½" RECTANGLES, (5) 2½" X 2½" SQUARES,

AND (2) 2 ½ " X 1 ½" RECTANGLES

SET THESE PIECES ASIDE.

2) USING THE 1½" STRIPS, SEW THE RIGHT SIDES TOGETHER FOR EACH OF THE FOLLOWING COMBINATIONS:

2 BROWN STRIPS TO 2 DARK GRAY STRIPS   1 DARK GRAY STRIP TO 1 LIGHT GRAY STRIP

CUT EACH OF THESE NEWLY COMBINED STRIPS IN HALF.

IRON EACH HALF OF THE STRIPS OPEN IN OPPOSITE DIRECTIONS. FOR EXAMPLE, IRON HALF OF THE DARK GRAY/LIGHT GRAY STRIP TOWARDS THE DARK GRAY AND THE OTHER HALF TOWARDS THE LIGHT GRAY. THESE NEW STRIPS SHOULD NOW MEASURE 2½" IN WIDTH.

3) TAKE THE DARK GRAY/LIGHT GRAY STRIPS AND NEST THE SEAMS (LINING THE SEAMS UP IN OPPOSITE DIRECTIONS TO ALLOW THE FABRIC TO LINE UP PERFECTLY) BY LAYING ONE RIGHT SIDE UP AND THE OTHER WRONG SIDE UP ON TOP OF IT. LINE YOUR STRIPS UP EVENLY AND TRIM THE EDGE.

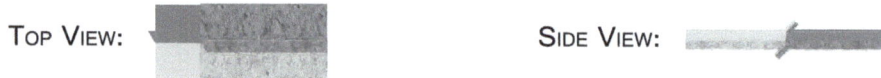

TOP VIEW: SIDE VIEW:

THEN CUT (4) SETS OF 2½" X 2½" SQUARES (8 TOTAL),   (3) SETS OF 2½" X 1½" RECTANGLES (6 TOTAL)

REPEAT THIS PROCESS FOR EACH SET OF STRIPS CUTTING:

BROWN/DARK GRAY - (10) SETS OF 2½" X 2½" SQUARES (20 TOTAL),

(3) SETS OF 2½" X 1½" RECTANGLES (6 TOTAL)

4) NOW IT IS TIME TO LAY OUT ALL OF THE PIECES. START WITH THE FIRST ROW AND LAY EACH PIECE RIGHT SIDE UP, MAKING SURE YOU PAY ATTENTION TO THE DIRECTION THE SEAM IS FACING. ALWAYS MAKE SURE THE SEAM IS FACING THE DIRECTION OF THE ARROW. IF THE SEAM IS FACING UP OR DOWN, MAKE SURE THAT THE PIECE NEXT TO IT IS NESTED (HAS THE SEAM IN THE OPPOSITE DIRECTION). RE-IRON ANY SEAMS THAT NEED TO BE CHANGED TO A DIFFERENT DIRECTION.

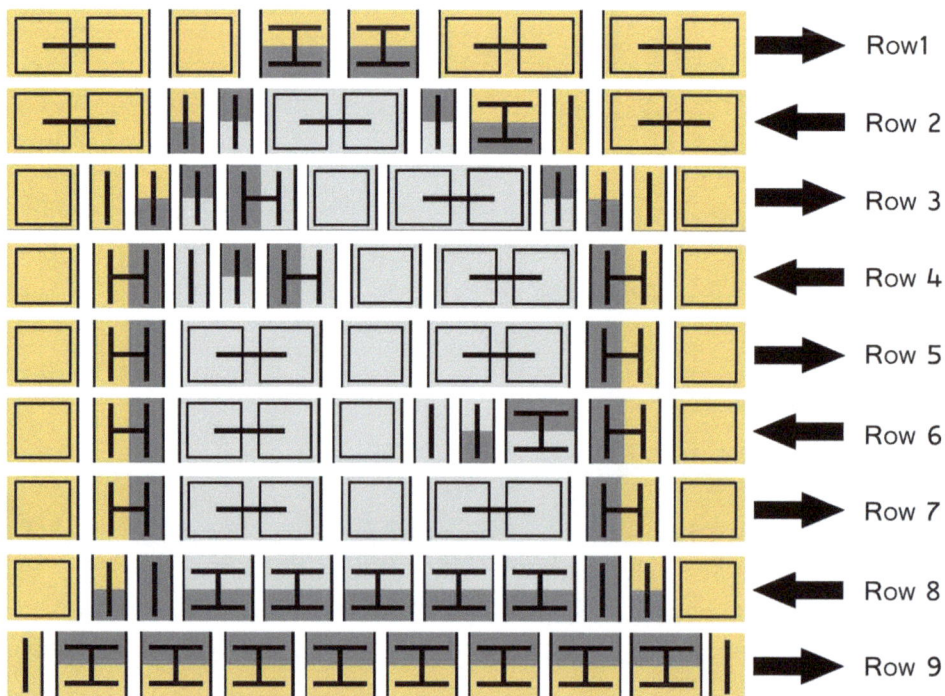

Row 1
Row 2
Row 3
Row 4
Row 5
Row 6
Row 7
Row 8
Row 9

5) Assemble each row, sewing right sides together and seams facing the direction of the arrow.

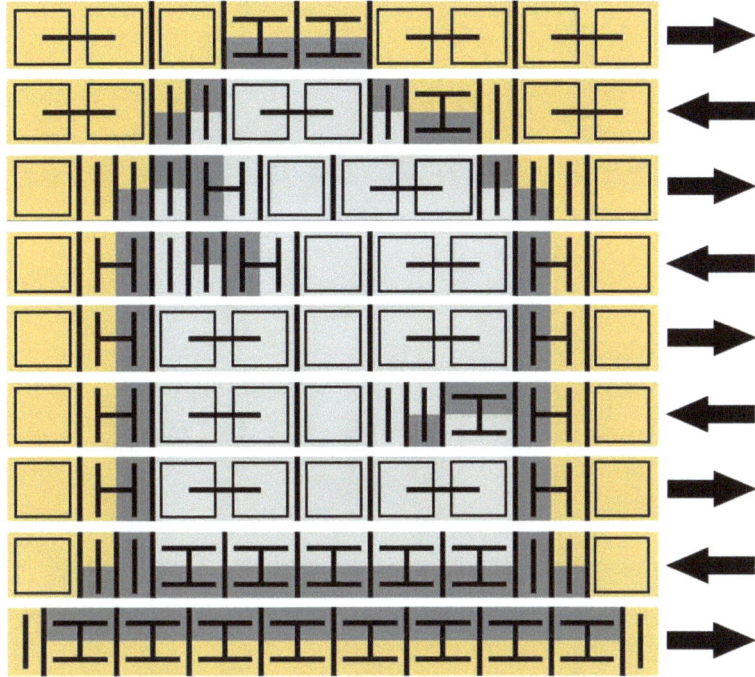

6) Sew the rows together, it does not matter which direction your seams point.

7) "Square" your block. Trim the edges of your block so they are even and your block is 18" by 18".

Pixelated Halloween Quilt Assembly

1) If you haven't yet squared your blocks, square them to 18 inches.

2) From your sashing fabric, cut 4 strips of 3½ inches. Cut these strips into 3½ by 18 inch strips.

3. Sew the 18 inch strips to the left and right side of your 4 center blocks (for sample layout blocks 2, 5, 8, and 11). Iron sashing away from blocks.

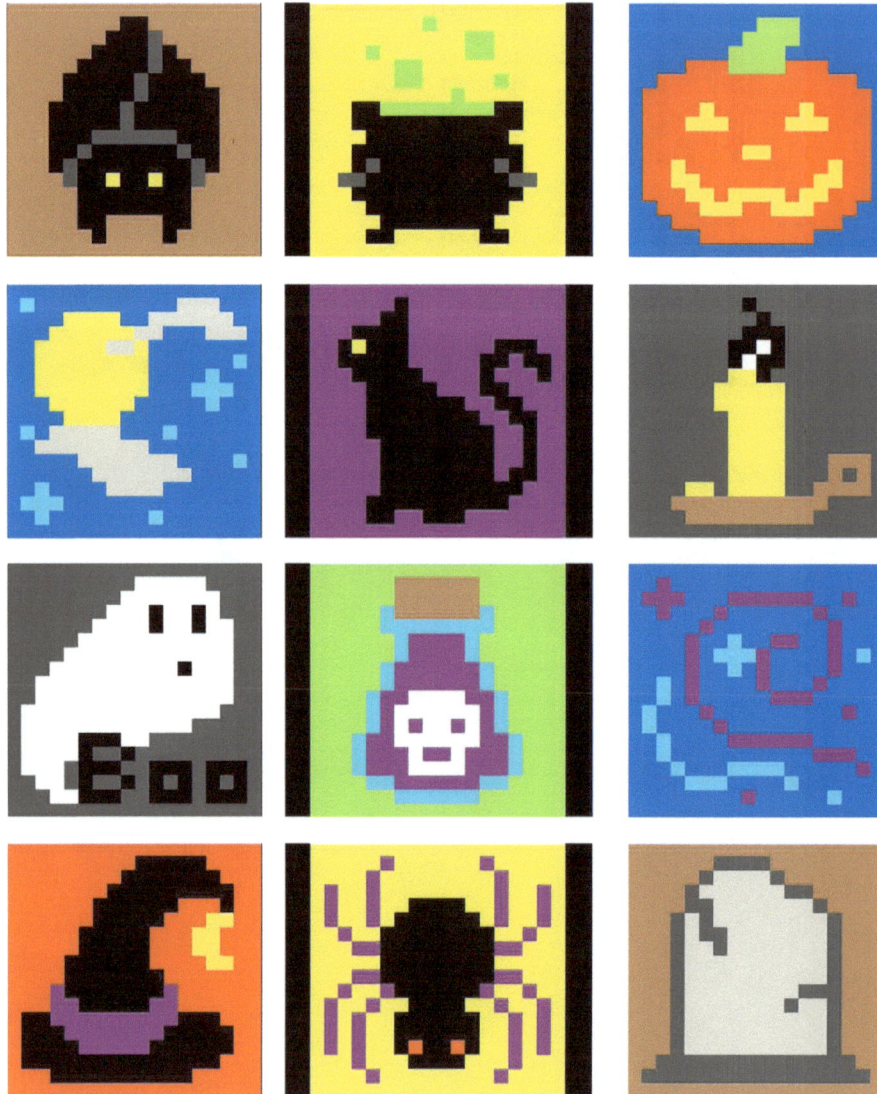

4) Sew the blocks on the left and right onto each center block. Iron the blocks away from the center block.

5) From the sashing fabric, cut 8 strips of 3½ inches. Cut 3 of these in half. Sew these ½ strips to the remaining 5 strips of fabric creating 5 strips of fabric at least 60 inches long. Cut these strips down to 3½ x 59 inches.

6) Sew a strip to the top and bottom of row 1. Sew the remaining 3 strips to bottom of each remaining row.

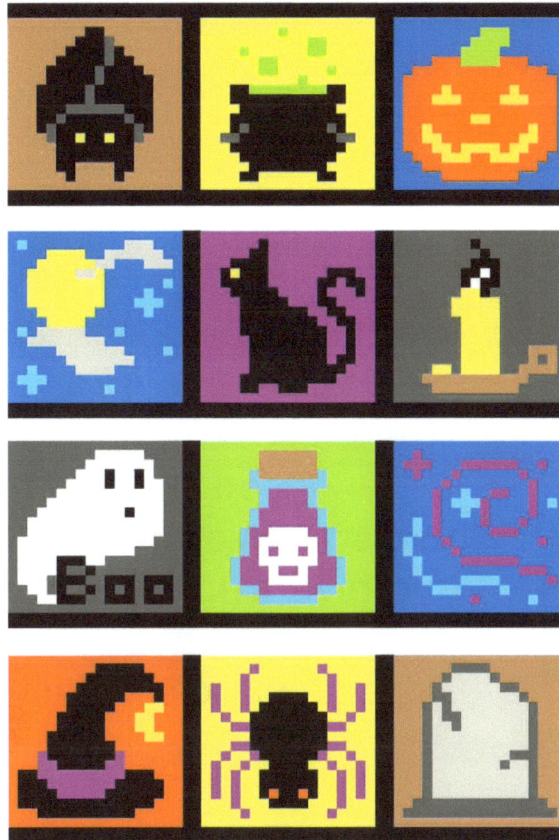

7) Sew the rows together.

8) From the sashing fabric cut 5 strips of 3½ inches. Cut 1 of these strips in half. Sew 2 sets of 2 strips plus a ½ strip together to create 2 strips over 100 inches long. Cut these strips down to 85 inches.

9) Sew the strips to the left and right of the quilt top.

10) Add any extra borders as you wish.

Toni has been selling her original comic book and video game quilts at conventions for years. Working with Nicole, their pattern line of pixelated quilts teach the basics of quilting, while showing experienced quilters new techniques. She also travels to teach classes, lecture, and give trunk shows. You can find her tutorials on YouTube or streaming live on Twitch under Quiltoni.

Nicole Ellison is a professional artist that has been working in the art world for over 15 years. She studied as an intern for a web design company during school before pursuing a degree in Studio Art. Since 2011, she has been running her own business as the Sole Proprietor of Craftigurumi where she specializes in creating unique handmade goods; such as plush toys, character dolls and cross stitch patterns. The Many Pieces Theory line of patterns is a joint creation between her and Toni where they combine Toni's quilting knowledge with Nicole's background in art and design.

www.ingramcontent.com/pod-product-compliance
Lightning Source LLC
Chambersburg PA
CBHW060820270326
41930CB00003B/105